DATE DUE

OCT 2 0 1997	

GAYLORD   PRINTED IN U.S.A.

THEORIES AND METHODS OF GROUP COUNSELING IN THE SCHOOLS

THEORIES AND METHODS OF GROUP COUNSELING IN THE SCHOOLS

Second Printing

Edited by

GEORGE M. GAZDA, Ed.D.

Professor of Education
University of Georgia
Athens, Georgia
and
Professor, Department of Psychiatry and Neurology
Medical College of Georgia
Augusta, Georgia

CHARLES C THOMAS • PUBLISHER

Springfield · Illinois · U.S.A.

Published and Distributed Throughout the World by

CHARLES C THOMAS • PUBLISHER

Bannerstone House

301-327 East Lawrence Avenue, Springfield, Illinois, U.S.A.

Natchez Plantation House

735 North Atlantic Boulevard, Fort Lauderdale, Florida, U.S.A.

© 1969, *by* CHARLES C THOMAS • PUBLISHER

ISBN 0-398-00660-1

Library of Congress Catalog Card Number: 78-77926

First Printing, 1969
Second Printing, 1972

*With THOMAS BOOKS careful attention is given to all details of
manufacturing and design. It is the Publisher's desire to present books that are
satisfactory as to their physical qualities and artistic possibilities and
appropriate for their particular use. THOMAS BOOKS will be true to those
laws of quality that assure a good name and good will.*

Printed in the United States of America

R-1

CONTRIBUTORS

JOHN D. BLAKEMAN, ED.D., *Assistant Professor of Education, Department of Counselor Education and Personnel Services, University of Georgia, Athens, Georgia.*

WARREN C. BONNEY, PH.D., *Professor of Education and Chairman, Department of Counselor Education and Personnel Services, University of Georgia, Athens, Georgia.*

SHERMAN R. DAY, ED.D., *Assistant Professor of Education, Department of Counseling and Educational Psychology, Georgia State College, Atlanta, Georgia.*

JONELL H. FOLDS, ED.D., *Associate Professor, Counseling and Guidance Division of Clinical Studies, College of Human Resources and Education, University of West Virginia, Morgantown, West Virginia.*

DANIEL W. FULLMER, PH.D., *Professor of Educational Psychology, University of Hawaii, Honolulu, Hawaii.*

GEORGE M. GAZDA, ED.D., *Professor of Education, Department of Counselor Education and Personnel Services, University of Georgia, Athens, Georgia; Professor of Psychiatry, Department of Psychiatry and Neurology, Medical College of Georgia, Augusta, Georgia.*

CLARENCE A. MAHLER, PH.D., *Professor of Psychology and Chairman of the Department of Psychology, Chico State College, Chico, California.*

BARBARA B. VARENHORST, PH.D., *Consulting Psychologist, Palo Alto Unified School District, Palo Alto, California.*

To my brothers
Thomas, Andrew, Lawrence, and Charles

PREFACE

T HIS BOOK IS designed for the school counselor. It is designed to provide him with a rationale and method for using group counseling at all grade levels in education and, in addition, a chapter was included to assist him in using group counseling with parents. The editor takes the position that the methods and, to some extent, the rationale for group counseling must vary with the age level and maturity of the counselee. For the preschool and early school child, play and action techniques with mixed-sex groups are emphasized; for the preadolescent, a different level of play, more appropriate to the age level, is involved and homogenous grouping with regard to sex is recommended; and for the adolescent and adult, interview group counseling is the treatment of choice. Variations of this "developmental approach" to group counseling also are described, especially for those counselees that are on the borderline of various age groups.

The basic purpose of this book is to give the student of group counseling and the practicing group counselor a theoretically sound as well as a comprehensive method of group counseling for the school setting. The book is intended as a textbook for courses in group counseling theory and procedures, and as such each author was asked, and for the most part complied, to address himself to the following areas: theoretical foundations of the position, including a description of how the process produces change (supported with research whenever possible); goals of the treatment; uniqueness of the treatment; counselor(s) role(s); client roles; qualifications of the counselor; composition of the group, including ages, problem types, and preferred number; limitations of the treatment; sample protocols, where they would add clarity; and suggested readings.

Each chapter contributor was selected because of his expertise with a particular approach to group counseling, and because of his current work with school counselors and group counseling in the schools. The positions described in this text are, of course, also appropriate for use by others than school counselors, who work in the helping professions within the school setting. School psychologists, psychiatric social workers, clinical psychologists and others with appropriate training and experience should find this text a useful guide.

Chapter I was included to show the history and development of group counseling and to illustrate the contributions to it by related disciplines. Significant contributors to group counseling and their contributions are also cited in this chapter. A general framework for group counseling in the schools was established in Chapter I.

Chapter II gives the group counselor a rationale for using small group action methods as the prime medium for children between the ages of five to ten or eleven. Other group procedures for this age group, in addition to group counseling, are also described in Chapter II. Chapters II and III represent a continuum along which play and action techniques are emphasized; whereas Chapter II emphasizes the use of the natural medium of play as the communication and therapeutic medium, Chapter III emphasizes play and activities of a higher order and usually in same-sexed groups. Activity Group Counseling, described by Blakeman and Day in Chapter III, utilizes many of the premises of Activity Group Therapy, but they have made modifications appropriate to the clientele and setting.

Chapters IV, V, and VI were selected to represent three major group counseling positions applicable to the adolescent and adult. Mahler's eclectic position (Chapter IV) contains within it considerable insights from practical experience in working with high school students, college students, and adults, although his emphasis in terms of procedures is on the high-school student.

Varenhorst, in Chapter V, describes the rationale and procedures of group counseling from a behavioral point of view. Although these procedures are applicable to different age levels, her emphasis, like Mahler's, is on the use of group counseling with high school youth.

Bonney develops his group counseling position, in Chapter

VI, around group dynamics principles with an emphasis on certain growth sequences or developmental stages in the life of a group. His position provides a third point of view for using group counseling with adolescents and adults.

The final chapter was chosen to present the theoretical rationale and methods for working with a special group of individuals involved in the problems of the school child—namely his parents, teachers and other school personnel, and siblings. There are occasions when the most therapeutic and expeditious method of treatment would be some form of family group counseling. One such position is Fullmer's Family Group Consultation (Chapter VII) which has particular merit for use in the school setting.

Theories and Methods of Group Counseling in the Schools was developed to improve the counselor's understanding and practice of group counseling in educational settings. It is my wish, as editor, that the efforts of each contributor to this text will improve group counseling services for the ultimate benefit of our youth.

For those who wish to study group counseling and therapy procedures which extend beyond the clientele and accommodations of educational settings, two earlier books by this editor, also published by Charles C Thomas are available. They are *Basic Approaches to Group Psychotherapy and Group Counseling* (1968), and *Innovations to Group Psychotherapy* (1968).

ACKNOWLEDGMENTS

To Jack, Sherm, Jonell, Clarence, Warren, Barbara, and Dan, my sincere appreciation first for your willingness to contribute to this text and, secondly, for your cooperation during the several processes of producing it. I would also like to thank the secretaries, Ethel Epps, Janet Sumpter, Linda Wilkes, and Sarah McDougal for their assistance with my correspondence concerning this text. I wish also to convey my deep sense of gratitude to Dr. Jack Duncan for his critical reading of the manuscript. And to my wife, Barbara, who typed the manuscript, and my son, David, who was patient with his father while he devoted time to this volume, my deepest appreciation.

G.M.G.

CONTENTS

THEORIES AND METHODS OF GROUP COUNSELING IN THE SCHOOLS

I

GROUP COUNSELING

Origin, Definition, and Contributing Disciplines and Individuals

GEORGE M. GAZDA

ORIGIN

T HE ORIGIN OF the term *group counseling* is somewhat obscured. Its historical antecedent was most likely group guidance or case conference. In other words, much like its counterpart, group psychotherapy, group counseling in its inception was very likely a class method similar to what is referred to today as *group guidance.* One of the earliest appearances in print in the United States of the term *group counseling* appears to have been in 1931. Dr. Richard D. Allen (1931), in an article titled "A Group Guidance Curriculum in the Senior High School" published in *Education,* used group counseling in the following context:

> *Group thinking and the case-conference method* usually take the place of the recitation. . . . Problems of educational and vocational guidance require teachers who are specially selected and trained for the work, who understand problems of individual differences and are continually studying them. These teachers require continuous contacts with the same pupils for several years, a knowledge of occupations and occupational problems, and special training in methods of individual and group counseling.
>
> All of these considerations draw attention to the class counselor as the logical teacher of the new unit. There is much similarity between the techniques of individual guidance and group guidance. When the counselor finds by individual interviews that certain problems are common to most of the pupils, such problems become units in the group guidance course. The class discussions of these problems should reduce the length and number of individual interviews with a saving of considerable time and expense. In fact, the

separation of group counseling from individual counseling would seem very short-sighted.

If the above principle prevails, the next serious problem concerns its practical application in the time schedule of the school. Ideally, such a course should be *extensive* rather than *intensive* in its nature, in order to accomplish its objectives effectively. Its purpose is to arouse interests in current educational, vocational and social problems, to develop social attitudes, and to build up a back-ground of occupational information. Such objectives require considerable *time extended over several years* (p. 190).[1]

This lengthy quotation is included to show that what Allen described as *group counseling* in 1931 is generally referred to as *group guidance* in 1969. Also it should be noted that Allen used the terms *case-conference, group guidance,* and *group counseling* interchangeably.

Although Allen's use of *group counseling* appeared in print in 1931, it is quite possible that he had used the expression before 1931. For example, John M. Brewer (1937), writing the Introduction to Allen's *Organization and Supervision of Guidance in Public Education,* published in 1937, wrote, "For more than a decade his colleagues in the Harvard Summer School have urged Dr. Allen to put his ideas into permanent form" (xxi).

Jones, as early as 1934, in his second edition of *Principles of Guidance,* states, "It [group guidance] is a term that has come into use chiefly through the excellent work of Richard T. D. Allen in Providence, R. I. It includes all those forms of guidance activities that are undertaken in groups or in classes" (1934, p. 284). Jones (1934, p. 291) also refers to the "Boston Plan for Group Counseling in Intermediate Schools" and cites the source as two circulars developed by the Committee on Guidance of the Boston Public Schools: Boston Public Schools, Guidance—Educational and Vocational, A Tentative Plan for Group Counseling, Board of Superintendents' Circular No. 2, 1928-1929 and Board of Superintendents' Circular No. 17, 1928-1929, First Supplement to Board of Superintendents' Circular No. 2. Boston:

---

[1] From Allen, R. D.: A group guidance curriculum in the senior high school. *Education,* 1931, *52,* 189-194. Reprinted from the October, 1931, issue of *Education,* by permission of the publishers, the Bobbs-Merrill Company, Inc.

Printing Department, 1929. Although group counseling is used in the title of the Boston publication, the description of the nature of the process described by Jones places it squarely in the realm of group guidance and not group counseling as it is defined today.

In his fifth edition of *Principles of Guidance,* published in 1963, Jones had this to say about Allen's case conference procedures: "A technique that combined the techniques of counseling in groups and group counseling was used by Allen and practiced in the public schools of Providence, Rhode Island more than twenty-five years ago" (1963, pp. 218-219). Jones believed that the purpose of the case conference was to provide the counselor with a means for students to discuss their personal and social relationships. Common problems of group members were used as the basis for discussion. A case was presented to the group to illustrate the problem, and each student was expected to compare his own experiences with those revealed through the case. The leader encouraged the group to seek the "more permanent values" exposed rather than the more "immediate temporary" ones, and he also encouraged the participants to consider the effect upon others of their proposed action. Conclusions were summarized to formulate generalizations for other situations. Jones stated that Allen believed his method worked best when "each case represented a common, usual, or typical situation that concerned most of the group. The case should involve persons and personal or social relations" (Jones, 1963, p. 219).

According to Jones, Allen characterized the case conference leader as one who never expressed approval or disapproval of any opinion or attitude and never stated opinions of his own. In addition, the leader was impartial and open-minded and encouraged the expression of all points of view; he would occasionally restate and summarize the group thinking, and organize the group so that it was large enough to guarantee a diversity of opinions, but not so large as to prevent each member the opportunity to enter into discussion.

The goals and procedures of Allen's case conference approach described by Jones are similar to those of contemporary group counselors; however, most contemporary group counselors do not structure their groups around specific cases.

DEFINITION

Although group counseling is likely here to stay—witness its inclusion in the *Review of Educational Research, Psychological Abstracts, Education Index* and similar indexes and references— it was not without substantial opposition. A brief tracing of the resistance to its acceptance is outlined below through the use of selected quotations. One of the first indications of impending opposition was revealed in the publication of "Revision of Principles of Vocational Guidance" in *The Vocational Guidance Magazine,* authored by deSchweinitz, Bradshaw, Buchwald, and Hayes (1929). This article equates group counseling with the giving of occupational information.

> The study of the general and local occupations, vocational opportunities and the problems of the occupational world should be carried on in organized classes, for all students in junior and senior high schools, continuation schools, evening schools, and colleges. It should give the student an acquaintance with the school unit in which he is, with the forms of higher education, the entire field of occupations and a method of studying occupations wherewith he can meet future vocational problems. Such classes should be given in appropriate years, especially preliminary to times of choice of courses, entrance upon a new school unit and to decision in regard to withdrawal from school . . . (1929, pp. 221-222).[2]

In his second edition of *Principles of Guidance,* Jones (1934) wrote, "Counseling has such an intimate sound, that it would seem advisable to limit it to that intimate, heart-to-heart talk between teacher and pupil. It is frankly admitted that it is difficult to draw the line sharply between the essence of what is done in the personal interview and what is done in small groups. But it is even more difficult to make any distinction

---

[2] From de Schweinitz, D.; Buchwald, L., and Hayes, M. H. S.: Revision of principles of vocational guidance. *Vocational Guidance Magazine,* 1929, 7, 218-226. Courtesy *The Personnel and Guidance Journal,* American Personnel and Guidance Association, Washington, D. C.

between group counseling and the more modern forms of class work. . ." (p.274).

Almost twenty years later, in his fifth edition of the same text, Jones (1963) wrote, "The values of group guidance are generally accepted, but the term 'group counseling' is still rejected by many guidance authorities. Some believe that group counseling is an 'anomaly' and say that it is as silly to speak of 'group counseling' as 'group courtship'" (pp. 217-218).

In the thirty-seventh yearbook of the National Society for the Study of Education, Part I "Guidance in Educational Institutions," Gilbert Wrenn (1938) wrote, "First of all, counseling is personal. It cannot be performed with a group. 'Group counseling' is a tautology; counseling is always personal" (p. 119). And in 1942, Brewer, also a highly respected guidance authority, wrote, "'Group guidance' was invented, apparently, as a term to mean classroom study, recitation, or discussion; is it any longer needed? 'Group counseling' is a similar term, but might it not be best to confine the word counseling to work with individuals?" (p. 294).

Slavson (1964), too, resists the use of the term group counseling. He states, "Counseling should be done on a one-to-one relation" (p. 102). He also believes that there are different treatments for different levels of the person's psyche. On the continuum from least to most in terms of depth and intensity of treatment and level of psyche reached, Slavson places group counseling at the level of least depth and intensity and most superficial level of psyche dealt with, and group psychotherapy at the level of greatest depth and intensity and deepest level of psyche reached. Group guidance lies in the middle of this continuum. In terms of duration of treatment, the order from shortest to longest is group counseling, group guidance, and group psychotherapy. Slavson's conception of group counseling and his placement of it on the above continuum is not in accord with the majority of group counselors. Goldman's (1962) placement in terms of content and process probably best represents the majority. He places group guidance at the least intense end of the continuum and group counseling in the middle, with group psychotherapy at the most intense level or greatest depth-of-treatment-end of the continuum.

Lifton (1966) also has dealt with the confusion of "group" terminology (including group counseling) and recently concluded "that although some nine years have passed since the earlier edition of this text was written, confusion and disagreement over the meaning of terms still exist" (p. 13). A "group procedures" interest group of some thirty members of the American Personnel and Guidance Association met at the Association's 1966 Convention in Washington, D.C., and appeared to confirm Lifton's conclusion when they had difficulty differentiating between group guidance and group counseling.[3]

To further confuse the issue, the term *multiple counseling* has been introduced by Froehlich (n.d.). Froehlich's use of mutiple counseling is consistent with the generally accepted use of *group counseling;* however, Helen Driver (1958) introduced multiple counseling to mean the conjunctive use of individual counseling with group counseling. Still others frequently use multiple counseling when they are referring to the use of more than one counselor.

Granted the confusion over the definition of group counseling, there is evidence that it is abating. A recent survey of fifty-four of the more prominent contributors to the field of group counseling for the period 1960 to 1965 revealed that 80 per cent preferred the term *group counseling* to *group guidance, multiple counseling, group therapy, psychodrama,* and *sociodrama* when they were asked to select the term which they preferred to use to describe "counseling with more than one individual simultaneously" (Gazda, Duncan, and Meadows, 1967). This appears consistent with a conclusion reached by Bennett as early as 1963. She states, "The term group counseling has become very popular, and practices under this name have been introduced rather widely in school systems. One might almost call it an epidemic" (1963, p. 136).

Forty-three of the respondents to the survey by Gazda, *et al.* (1967) (i.e., those who preferred the term group counseling)

---

[3] Personal communication.

were asked to define it. From their definitions, the following composite definition was generated.

> Group counseling is a dynamic interpersonal process focusing on conscious thought and behavior and involving the therapy functions of permissiveness, orientation to reality, catharsis, and mutual trust, caring, understanding, acceptance, and support. The therapy functions are created and nurtured in a small group through the sharing of personal concerns with one's peers and the counselor(s). The group counselees are basically normal individuals with various concerns which are not debilitating to the extent requiring extensive personality change. The group counselees may utilize the group interaction to increase understanding and acceptance of values and goals and to learn and/or unlearn certain attitudes and behaviors (Gazda, *et al.*, 1967, p. 306).[4]

The above definition was constructed in a fashion similar to Gustad's (1953) definition of individual counseling. Both definitions stress the *learning* emphasis of the counseling relationship and both are by construction eclectic.

Group counseling and group psychotherapy lie on a continuum with an overlapping of goals and professional competencies, but the subtle distinctions are evident in expressions such as "basically normal" counselees "focusing on conscious thought and behavior," and "concerns which are not debilitating to the extent requiring extensive personality change," found in references to group *counseling*.

Brammer and Shostrom have conceptualized the differences quite pointedly through the use of a series of adjectives wherein counseling is described as "educational, supportive, situational, problem-solving, conscious awareness, emphasis on 'normals,' and short-term. Psychotherapy is characterized by supportive (in a more particular sense), reconstructive, depth analysis, analytical, focus on the unconscious, emphasis on 'neurotics' or other severe emotional problems, and long-term" (1960, p. 6). Although Brammer and Shostrom are describing individual counseling and psychotherapy, respectively, these differentiations also would

---

[4] From Gazda, G. M.; Duncan, J. A., and Meadows, M. E.: Counseling and group procedures: Report of a survey. *Counselor Education and Supervision,* 1967, 6, 305-310. Courtesy of *Counselor Education and Supervision.*

seem to be applicable to group counseling and group psychotherapy.

Attempts to differentiate between counseling or therapy
groups and other types of group processes have been made by
Goldman (1962), Coffey (1952), and Glanz (1962). Goldman
(1962) seemed to be concerned primarily with distinguishing
between guidance and counseling groups; his differentiation
between counseling and therapy groups is not so clear-cut. Goldman contends that groups must be viewed in light of "content"
and "process" and their interaction. Content of guidance groups
consists of school-related topics, *e.g.*, how to study, choosing a
college, etc., whereas content for a counseling group may include
the same topics, in addition to other nonschool topics, *e.g.*,
dating behavior, parent-child relations, and the like. Process
refers to type of leadership and, to some extent, level of disturbance. In guidance groups there is more leader direction where
the emphasis is on cognitive elements, whereas in counseling
and therapy groups the topics originate with the participants
and feelings and needs are emphasized. Goldman's paradigm for
differentiating between guidance and counseling groups through
the concepts of "content" and "process" is quite useful in clarifying their similarities and differences.

Coffey (1952), in referring to Jennings' (1950) "socio" and
"psyche" groups, describes therapy groups as typifying the psyche
process, and action groups, committees, and the like as examples
of socio process groups. The basic distinction between these
groups appears to be in their goals or purposes. The purpose
of the psyche group is the satisfaction of emotional needs of
group members, and the purpose of the socio groups is the completion of specified or "visualized" goals of the group. Coffey
refers to the socio group process as task-oriented and describes
groups as lying on a continuum between psyche and socio process,
rarely existing in "pure form" at either end of the continuum.
The satisfaction of emotional needs of group members through
psyche groups is consistent with the author's definition of group
counseling.

Still another fruitful method of conceptualizing differences between groups is to consider whether their function is task-centered or growth-centered. Glanz (1962) utilizes these functional differences to differentiate between therapy groups, "an extreme form of growth groups," and "action" groups—in which the primary function is to get a task completed—task-oriented. The author considers group counseling to be "growth" rather than "task-oriented."

In summary, group counseling may be described as growth-centered (psyche process) rather than task-centered (socio process). There is no *group* goal as such, but rather each member has his unique goal. The group counselor's role is that of encouraging open discussion of members' concerns, needs, and feelings and responding in a therapeutic fashion to the feelings of each member and the group feeling.

DISCIPLINES CONTRIBUTING TO GROUP COUNSELING

The previous reference to R. D. Allen's use of the term group counseling suggests that Allen may have coined the expression; however, the author does not contend that he has discovered the missing link. More likely than not, several individuals were using the term in Allen's era. Several other movements have also contributed to the group counseling movement. The most significant of these contributing movements were group psychotherapy, child guidance, vocational guidance, social casework, and group work.

Group Psychotherapy

Corsini (1957) has referred to group psychotherapy as "a conglomerate of methods and theories having diverse multiple origins in the past, resulting inevitably from social demands, and developed in various forms by many persons" (p. 9). J. L. Moreno (1966) contends that group psychotherapy has its roots in medicine, sociology, and religion. If we accept July 1, 1905 (Hadden, 1955), the date that J. H. Pratt introduced his "class method," as the beginning of group psychotherapy, rather than some ancient ritual such as Mesmer's group treatment through suggestion, the history of group psychotherapy covers approximately a mere sixty-five years.

The term *group therapy* was introduced by J. L. Moreno in 1931 (Z. Moreno, 1966), and *group psychotherapy* was introduced, also by J. L. Moreno, in 1932 (Corsini, 1957). For the most part, group therapy and group psychotherapy are used synonymously in current discourse; group therapy has become the shortened or colloquial version of group psychotherapy.

Even though the term group psychotherapy was not coined until 1932 by J. L. Moreno, an emigrant to America, there is considerable evidence that group psychotherapy is an American invention and that various forms were being practiced in the United States, mostly by psychiatrists and ministers, long before Moreno labeled the practice. Group therapy was coined by Moreno about the same time as the expression *group counseling* was used in the literature by R. D. Allen; however, there is every reason to believe that Allen's use of group counseling was more closely related to group instruction than was the meaning that Moreno intended when he coined group therapy and group psychotherapy.

Numerous systems of group psychotherapy were described in the professional literature well in advance of the professional literature, which is still quite meager, concerning group counseling. It is recognized, therefore, that group psychotherapy, as practiced and as described in the literature, provided much of the theoretical rationale for the emergence of group counseling. Just how much credit the group psychotherapy movement should receive for the emergence and development of group counseling is uncertain, but the writer believes it to be considerable, probably the most significant of the several disciplines or movements contributing to the emergence and growth of group counseling.

Child Guidance

The possibility exists that group counseling originated in Europe. Dreikurs and Corsini (1954) contend that between 1900 and 1930 major steps were being made in Europe toward a systematic use of the group method called "collective counseling" (sic). They believe that Alfred Adler, in his child guidance clinics in Vienna, was likely the first psychiatrist to use *collective counseling* formally and systematically.

Ansbacher and Ansbacher (1956) translated many of Adler's works, and in their commentary on his writing, they stated, "Although Adler himself never practiced group therapy, he suggested its use for the treatment of criminals" (p. 347). It is not because of his suggestion for using group therapy with criminals that Adler is considered by some to be the father of the movement, but rather because of his application of group techniques in his child guidance clinics. According to the Ansbachers, Adler was conducting group procedures—perhaps collective counseling—as early as 1922.

The rationale and methods employed by Adler and his followers are described by Ansbacher and Ansbacher (1956). However, the Ansbachers, because they were unable to find "more than a mere mention" of Adler's rationale and methods in his own writings, were forced to turn to secondary sources, *i.e.*, the writings of Seidler and Zilat, and Rayner and Holub. Seidler and Zilat described the "public" character of Adlerian child guidance clinics, for example, the child interviewed in the presence of an adult audience. Doris Rayner defends this form of treatment by stating that the child benefits because he comes to view his difficulty as a "community problem," and his audience (parents) receive an education in parent-child behavior. Martha Holub agreed with Rayner's position of the mutual therapeutic benefits to the child and adult through participation in this Adlerian "open-door" treatment procedure.

In 1942 Brewer described the child guidance movement "as yet largely dissociated from the work of the schools ..." (p. 263). Nevertheless, because of its many similarities, the child guidance movement *may* have influenced, directly or indirectly, the group counseling movement.

Vocational Guidance

Frank Parsons has been recognized as the father of the vocational guidance movement because of his founding of the Vocations Bureau of Boston in 1908 (Brewer, 1942). Just when, where, and by whom the word *group* was added to the word *guidance* is not known; however, according to Brewer (1942), Charles L. Jacobs of San Jose was one of the first to suggest a wider use of the term guidance when, in the October, 1915, issue of *Manual Training and Vocational Education,* he stated that his work included three departments—educational guidance, vocational guidance, and avocational guidance.

Classes in Occupational Information. As early as 1908, William A. Wheatley was instrumental in introducing a course in occupational information for freshman boys at Westport, Connecticut High School. Similar courses were offered in Boston and New York City soon after Wheatley's course (Brewer, 1942).

Homeroom. McKown (1934) authored a text, *Home Room Guidance,* as early as 1934. The content of the text and the fact that McKown proposed the director of guidance as the director of homeroom guidance suggest its close association to group guidance and counseling. In fact, some schools referred to the homeroom as "the 'guidance hour,' or 'guidance room'" (McKown, 1934, p. 53). In a publication of approximately the same vintage of McKown's, Strang (1935) cited the contribution of the homeroom teacher as being fourfold: "to establish friendly relationships, to discover the abilities and needs, and to develop right attitudes toward school, home, and community" (p. 116). Once more the group guidance and counseling "flavor" was expressed in the work of the homeroom teacher.

Extracurricular activities. C. R. Foster authored a book, *Extra Curricular Activities,* in 1925 in which he recognized guidance as an extracurricular activity. In the same text, Foster also urged the counselor to "hold many group conferences with the students on the subject of future educational or vocational plans" (p. 182). Pittsburgh was cited by Foster as including instructional guidance taking "the form of tenth grade group conferences which were held for the purpose of discussing Pittsburgh's industrial life and the opportunities it affords the young people" (1925, p. 183).

The vocational guidance movement was instrumental in the introduction of homeroom guidance, classes in occupational information, and certain extracurricular activities which were forerunners of current group guidance and group counseling.

Social Casework

In reviewing the history of the Marriage Council of Philadelphia, Gaskill and Mudd (1950) stated that group counseling and family life education had been part of the "Marriage Council's service from the agency's inception in 1932" (p. 194). Whether or not the term *group counseling* itself was actually used by the Council as early as 1932 and whether or not the treatment was similar to current group counseling is not indicated. However, Gaskill and Mudd (1950) gave the following definition of group counseling which they attributed to Hazel Froscher, Margery Klein, and Helen Phillips:

> . . . a dynamic relationship between a counselor and the members of a group; involving presentation and discussion of subjects about which the counselor has special knowledge, which is of general or specific concern to the group and around which emotions may be brought out and attitudes developed or changed. The relationship between the group members themselves and the counselor's use of this is essentially important in the total process (1950, p. 195).[5]

The definition implies that the counselor gives a presentation and encourages discussion of it. Gaskill and Mudd (1950), in their description of the group counseling session, indicate that the group ranged between thirty-five and fifty persons in size, and they further described the group sessions as a *course* including speakers other than the group counselor. This approach to group counseling seems more closely related to group guidance or a family living class rather than the typical small, eight to ten-member counseling groups where leader-imposed content is absent or minimal.

Group Work

Sullivan (1952) described a group in the following manner:

> . . . The group must be a small stable one which feels itself as an entity and which the individual can feel close identification. Membership . . . is voluntary. There is a group leader, who is consciously making constructive use of the process of personality

---

[5] From Gaskill, E., and Mudd, E.: A decade of group counseling. *Social Casework*, 1950, *31*, 194-201. Courtesy of *Social Casework*.

interaction among the members. The leader utilizes the desire of a normal person to be accepted by his fellows. He establishes the dignity of the individual and teaches acceptance of differences in race, creed, and nationality. Group work stresses programs evolved by the group itself, in consultation with the leader who guides toward socially desirable ends. Creative activities are encouraged to provide legitimate channels of self-expressions and to relieve emotional stress. Competition for its own sake is minimized and group members learn from situations where cooperation brings rich satisfaction. The trained leader arranges for leadership practice by group members; individual responsibility and group responsibility grow as the group takes on new functions. The atmosphere is friendly, informal, and democratic (p. 189).[6]

This description of group work contains many of the ingredients that are present in definitions of group counseling, and the possible influence on group counseling of the group work specialists becomes readily apparent.

SIGNIFICANT CONTRIBUTORS

For one to attempt to cite some of the most significant contributors to the speciality of group counseling while living in the era of the beginning of the movement is to court professional suicide; nevertheless, an attempt will be made to sketch briefly the author's perception of those who have been and, in most instances, are still making significant contributions to the group counseling movement. The author concluded that the leaders of the group counseling movement are citizens of the United States, and this assumption seems supported by Brewer (1942). If this conclusion is erroneous, it might at least stimulate others to investigate and challenge it.

The credit for coining the term group counseling may be attributed to Richard D. Allen, although there is no absolute proof of this. Others who were among the first to publish and teach in the field of group counseling were Margaret Bennett, Ruth Strang, and Jane Warters. Evelyn Gaskill and Emily Mudd should be cited for their early use of group counseling in social

---

[6] From Sullivan, D. F. *Readings in Group Work*, New York, Association Press, 1952. Courtesy of Association Press, New York.

casework, Hanna Grunwald for the current appplication of group counseling in case work agencies, and Joseph Knowles for his successful application of the group approach to pastoral counseling.

Clifford Froehlich and Helen Driver have influenced the group counseling movement with their introduction of multiple counseling, and E. Wayne Wright, upon the death of Froehlich, has become one of the leading proponents for the multiple counseling emphasis of the movement.

Merle Ohlsen, Fred Proff, and several of their colleagues and students at the University of Illinois, the author among them, are known for their early attempt to research group counseling. Ben Cohn, who was influenced by Ohlsen, and his associates of the Board of Cooperative Educational Services of Bedford Hills, New York, researched the effects of group counseling on acting-out adolescents. Stanley Caplan did research with similar groups.

Norman Kagan is also adding new information to the field through his recent research efforts, as is Charles Truax and associates. Clarence Mahler and Edson Caldwell coauthored one of the first texts on group counseling in the schools, and Mahler has since authored a second group counseling book.

Among those representing the various schools of group counseling are Walter Lifton, Thomas Gordon, and Nicholas Hobbs—three of the most prominent proponents of the client-centered approach to group counseling. Rudolf Dreikurs, Manford Sonstegard, and Donald Dinkmeyer are among the most significant Adlerian-oriented contributors to the field of group counseling, While John Krumboltz, Barbara Varenhorst, and Carl E. Thoresen are making their place with a behavior-oriented application of group counseling. Warren Bonney and his students have pioneered in the application of group dynamics principles and concepts to group counseling, and Betty Berzon has championed self-directed and instrumented or programmed counseling groups and studied group process and climate.

Dan Fullmer and Harold Bernard have introduced to the field, elsewhere and in this text, *Family Group Consultation*, and Blakeman and Day have described, also in this text, an activity group counseling approach for use with preadolescents and adolescents.

Dwight Arnold, G. Edward Stormer, C. G. Kemp, and the author currently are developing an "interest group" among the American Personnel and Guidance Association members for the purpose of defining the field, sharing information on training programs, and establishing communication among practitioners to provide some form of organization to the loose-knit movement. In an attempt to establish the present status of the movement and to arrive at a definition of group counseling, the author and his former students Duncan and Meadows have surveyed recent contributors to the field of group counseling and the results have been published in *Counselor Education and Supervision*, Summer 1967.

Even as this chapter is being written, significant contributions are being made by persons unknown to the author, and because of the explosion of interest in the field of group procedures and group counseling and as a result of the publication lag, many persons will be well established in this speciality whose names will not appear in this chapter on its publication date.

SUMMARY

This chapter traces the history of the development of group counseling by attempting to establish the person(s) who were responsible for coining the term and the related disciplines contributing to its growth and development. Illustrations of resistance to its development are also described.

Confusion over the definition of group counseling is outlined, and group counseling is then defined as well as contrasted with other related group procedures.

The related disciplines found to have contributed to the evolution and development of group counseling include group psychotherapy, child guidance, vocational guidance, social casework, and group work. These disciplines and the manner in which they have most likely influenced group counseling are systematically described.

The chapter closes with an enumeration of some of the

more prominent contributors to group counseling, including a brief description of the nature of their contribution.

REFERENCES

Allen, R. D.: A group guidance curriculum in the senior high school. *Education,* 1931, *52,* 189-194.

Ansbacher, H. L., and Ansbacher, R. R. (Eds.): *The Individual Psychology of Alfred Adler.* New York: Basic Books, 1956.

Bennett, M. C.: *Guidance and Counseling in Groups.* (2nd ed.) New York: McGraw, 1963.

Brammer, L. M., and Shostrom, E. L.: *Therapeutic Psychology.* Englewood Cliffs, N. J.: Prentice Hall, 1960.

Brewer, J. M.: Introduction. In R. D. Allen (Ed.): *Organization and Supervision of Guidance in Public Education.* New York: Inor, 1937. pp. xxi-xxii.

Brewer, J. M.: *History of Vocational Guidance.* New York: Harper, 1942.

Coffey, H. S.: Socio and psyche group process: Integrative concepts. *Journal of Social Issues,* 1952, *8,* 65-74.

Corsini, R. J.: *Methods of Group Psychotherapy.* Chicago: William James Press, 1957.

de Schweinitz, D.; Bradshaw, F.; Buchwald, L., and Hayes, M. H. S.: Revision of principles of vocational guidance. *Vocational Guidance Magazine,* 1929, *7,* 218-226.

Dreikurs, R., and Corsini, R. J.: Twenty years of group psychotherapy. *American Journal of Psychiatry,* 1954, *110,* 567-575.

Driver, H. I.: *Counseling and Learning in Small-group Discussion.* Madison, Wisc.: Monona, 1958.

Foster, C. R.: *Extra-curricular Activities in the High School.* Richmond, Va.: Johnson, 1925.

Froehlich, C. P.: Multiple counseling—A research proposal. Berkeley: University of California Department of Education, n.d.

Gaskill, E. R., and Mudd, E. H.: A decade of group counseling. *Social Casework,* 1950, *31,* 194-201.

Gazda, G. M.; Duncan, J. A., and Meadows, M. E.: Counseling and group procedures—Report of a survey. *Counselor Education and Supervision,* 1967, *6,* 305-310.

Glanz, E. C.: *Groups in Guidance.* Boston: Allyn & Bacon, 1962.

Goldman, L.: Group guidance, content and process. *Personnel and Guidance Journal,* 1962, *40,* 518-522.

Gustad, J. W.: The definition of counseling. In R. F. Berdie (Ed.): *Roles and relationships in counseling.* Minnesota Studies in Student Personnel Work, No. 3, Minneapolis: University of Minnesota Press, 1953.

Hadden, S. B.: Historic background of group psychotherapy. *International Journal of Group Psychotherapy,* 1955, 5, 162-168.

Jennings, H. H.: *Leadership and Isolation.* (2nd ed.) New York: Longmans, Green, 1950.

Jones, A. J.: *Principles of Guidance,* (2nd ed.) New York: McGraw-Hill, 1934.

Jones, A. J.: *Principles of Guidance,* (5th ed.) New York: McGraw-Hill, 1963.

Lifton, W. M.: Working with groups. (2nd ed.) New York: Wiley, 1966.

McKowan, H. C.: *Home Room Guidance.* New York: McGraw-Hill, 1934.

Moreno, J. L. (Ed.): *The International Handbook of Group Psychotherapy.* New York: Philosophical Lib., 1966.

Moreno, Z. T.: Evolution and dynamics of the group psychotherapy movement. In J. L. Moreno (Ed.): *The International Handbook of Group Psychotherapy.* New York: Philosophical Lib., 1966. pp. 27-125.

Slavson, S. R.: *A Textbook in Analytic Group Psychotherapy.* New York: International University Press, 1964.

Strang, R.: *The Role of the Teacher in Personnel Work.* New York: Bureau of Publications, Teachers College, Columbia University, 1935.

Sullivan, D. F. (Ed.): *Readings in Group Work.* New York: Association Press, 1952.

Wrenn, C. G.: Counseling with students. In G. M. Whipple (Ed.): Guidance in educational institutions, Part I. *National Society for the Study of Education.* Bloomington, Ill.: Public School Publishing Co., 1938, pp. 119-143.

II

GROUP PROCEDURES IN THE ELEMENTARY SCHOOL

GEORGE M. GAZDA AND JONELL H. FOLDS

T HE TITLE FOR this chapter indicates that there is more than the interview-type counseling approach to working with children in groups. To speak of group procedures rather than group counseling seems more appropriate because many of the elements of group counseling are also elements common in varying degrees to the other group procedures described in this chapter—namely group guidance, sociodrama, psychodrama, play techniques, and play therapy. The rationale for working with children in the elementary school age group, which is presented in this chapter, is based on some of the procedures which have been more often referred to as therapy than counseling.

Since school personnel generally are reluctant to practice *therapy*, and rightly so, they have as a result also failed to utilize therapeutic procedures which are appropriate for use by teachers and counselors in the school setting. Under the circumstances, considerable liberty has been taken with the outline and contents of this chapter, since it does describe group procedures which are currently used with elementary school children as well as other group procedures (with suggested modifications) which heretofore have had limited use as a part of the guidance and counseling armamentarium of elementary school teachers and counselors. It differs also from the other chapters in this book in that it includes a survey of the activities and procedures used in working with young children as well as the authors' own developing position which they feel to be most consistent with the concept of developmental task with emphasis on action

21

methods which are described with principles or concepts of learning. These action methods, explained through learning principles, may, in fact, be closely related to "game theory."

The concept of developmental tasks gives the guidance and counseling specialist a framework around which to conceptualize the guidance and counseling needs for each age group within the elementary school, and the utilization of play techniques and sociodramatic and psychodramatic procedures capitalizes on the general receptivity of the elementary school child to play and action. Although play and action are natural to the child, the play materials and playroom for counseling use are not standard in most schools. For effective group counseling using these procedures, playrooms, play media, and storage facilities must be made available. Meeks (1967) calls attention to these needs, and recommends that the playroom, or "guidance suite" be soundproof and located apart from the classrooms and administrative offices. The procedures described in this chapter are appropriate for teachers and counselors working with children from kindergarten (age 5) to early adolescence (age 10-11).

RATIONALE FOR SMALL GROUP PROCEDURES

Children like to belong to groups, whether the purpose is self-determined or whether it is determined by adult or authority figures. In general, they respond to and assist each other in learning new skills, attitudes, and ways of relating through identifying, reflecting, questioning, and verbally or motorically responding. Their activities, whether in a planned or structured learning situation or in a spontaneous play group, are a part of real life, not separate from it. They are spontaneous, open, and impressionable. Thus planned group guidance activities designed to enhance their emotional, social, and creative development fit naturally into their mode of behaving and offer an effective procedure for preventing maladjustment.

The authors (Gazda and Folds, 1968) have developed for the purpose of implementing group guidance, the concept of critical incidents for the junior and senior high school age groups. This concept was developed to enable the guidance specialist to delimit and define the nature of guidance concepts which need to be provided for these age groups. Essentially, the contention of the authors is that there are certain needs (personal, social, educational, and vocational) that students possess and that are not systematically met in his regular academic courses within the school curriculum. The needs, therefore, should be defined and provided for through a systematic group guidance program. The program (Gazda and Folds, 1968) of guidance activities and group sessions which was developed to meet these needs consists of a series of twenty-one units within three major areas: Orientation (to the school), Personal Development, and Educational and Vocational Planning. Similarly, the elementary school child requires the careful attention to his developmental needs. For this age group, the concept of *developmental tasks,* popularized by Havighurst, (1948, 1953) provides the elementary school guidance specialists and teachers with insights into the *critical* guidance and counseling needs of this age group.

Developmental task is defined by Havighurst (1953) as

> . . . a task which arises at or about a certain period in the life of the individual, successful achievement of which leads to his happiness and to success with later tasks, while failure leads to unhappiness in the individual, disapproval by the society, and difficulty with later tasks (p. 2).[1]

The concept of developmental tasks seems especially appropriate as a framework around which to develop the application of group procedures to the child of elementary school years because it is during this early period that some of the most dramatic physical and psychological changes occur. Shaftel and Shaftel (1949) described the successful use of problem-stories based upon the developmental tasks of middle children and "critical conflict situations" from the child development literature as classroom warm-up technique for sociodrama; Zaccaria (1965) recommends the application of the concept to achieving the

---

[1] From Havighurst, R. J.: *Human development and education.* 1966. Reprinted by permission David McKay Company, Inc., New York, New York.

goals of guidance, and similarly, Blocher (1966) has integrated the concept in the development of an approach to counseling. If school personnel are to understand the developing child and meet his needs through the school curriculum and policies, they must be familiar with specific features of each stage of development and the required coping behavior of each child for the successful completion of the stage. Space does not permit a thorough discussion of the stages and tasks which all children encounter; however, these stages with concomitant tasks are described by Tryon and Lilienthal III (1950), Lilienthal III and Tryon (1950), Erickson (1950), Havighurst (1953), Brammer and Shostrom (1960), and more recently by Blocher (1966). Gessell and Ilg's (1964) *The Child from Five to Ten* is also an appropriate reference.

It is necessary to stress the point made by others (Gazda & Ohlsen, 1966; Levy, 1940; Solomon, 1955) that the young child is very much the slave of his environment or his *environmental presses,* particularly the adults who control much of his life. The editor of this volume vividly recalls expressions from a fifth-grade counseling group that emphasized their concept of the environment; *e.g.,* "We're just kids; we don't count!" "Our dogs get better treatment at home than we do!" "We're treated like dirt under their (parents') feet!" Expressions like these convey the feeling of lack of personal respect and lack of opportunity by the young child to make significant decisions or to control his environment. He may be at the mercy of his environment most of the time, and he often feels this helplessness. The elementary school counselor, therefore, must be willing to assist the child in the manipulation of his environment. The forms which this manipulation take are many and varied, but most often it will mean that the counselor will need to work with the adults who are responsible for controlling the child. These adults usually are the parents or parent surrogates and teachers. Thus, most professionals recommend that the elementary school counselor devote a considerable amount of his time to consulting with parents and teachers as an approach to preventing problem behavior of the elementary school child.

Hill (1967), in referring to the ACES-ASCA Committee on

the Elementary School Counselor and the report of the APGA
Committee on Dimensions of Elementary School Guidance,
cites the general agreement for a three-fold role (counseling—
consultation—coordination) of the elementary school counselor.
Patterson (1967) cautions that the elementary school child is
amenable to verbal methods of counseling and warns that counseling the child should be the significant function of the elementary school counselor.

This chapter emphasizes the prevention of problems through
group procedures that are particularly appropriate for use with
the child from nursery school through the first six grades. The
chapter in the text by Blakeman and Day emphasizes group
techniques appropriate for upper grade school children (junior
high school) and Fullmer's chapter emphasizes a method for
involving parents and teachers in small groups for the primary
purpose of assisting children in both of these age groups as
well as the adolescent. The age groups emphasized in the
chapters by Bonney, Mahler, and Varenhorst are senior high
school and college-age students; however, Varenhorst in particular, cites research involving behavioral group counseling with
children, adolescents, and adults.

GROUP GUIDANCE

In many ways, a group guidance experience is similar to
that of group counseling. A friendly, permissive, emotional
climate is common to both. There are differences, however,
which are basic to the objectives for the individual. Whereas
in group counseling, the focus of attention is on the issue which
has significance to the *individual* in the group; in group guidance,
the focus of attention is on the aspects of information and
discussion which are most relevant to the *group*. Thus, in group
guidance, both the process and content are more oriented to the
concerns of the group collectively than is true in group counseling.

In group guidance, the content is school related, *e.g.*, how
to study, choosing a college, etc., and the process includes leader
and group members collaborating for the purpose of providing
information to the student of the sort that might change his
attitude and opinion. On the other hand, in group counseling

the content can be both school related, as cited above, and nonschool related, *e.g.*, dating behavior, parent-child relations, etc., which originate with group members; the process includes free discussion, role playing, etc., and feelings and needs are emphasized (Goldman, 1962).

Group procedures with children which are primarily guidance in nature, as opposed to therapeutic, are those which emphasize the informative and cognitive elements rather than the affective elements. As mentioned previously, guidance and counseling overlap and guidance overlaps also with teaching—the process of guidance being somewhere between the two. The activities which have been employed with elementary school pupils and the objectives and outcomes of the activities demonstrate a varied approach to guidance. Some of the guidance activities which seem to be most effective in working with young children are presented in the following brief review of the related literature.

Studies of Group Guidance Activities

Davis (1958) reported positive results in his experiment to modify children's reaction to school tasks through a puppet play teaching technique. The puppets were used to dramatize different behavior toward a study task. The subjects were kindergarten-level children, and the experiment was performed by the teachers. He concluded that the puppet lessons "contributed to verbal identification of specific behavior reactions that are negatively related to accomplishment of school tasks" and that the technique is "a valuable asset in a group environment." Davis suggests applying the technique to a wide range of behavior problems in the school, such as taking turns, sharing, listening skills, and so forth.

Bender and Woltmann (1936) in a discussion of the use of puppet shows and puppet classes as a psychotherapeutic method for working with behavior problems in children call it a "most valuable" activity. The children with whom they worked seemed to respond more freely in groups than alone. The children were encouraged by the presence of other children with mutual experiences. Bender and Woltmann also felt that the activities centering around puppet classes (i.e., making puppets, writing plays, drawing puppet characters, and witnessing or producing puppet plays) had a therapeutic effect. Puppet shows apparently allow the child to express his own world.

Motion pictures were used by Denny (1958) in an attempt to reduce frustration in eighth-grade pupils. He found the activity successful and recommended using this technique with pupils in other grade levels and experimenting with using motion pictures under different time situations and with juvenile delinquents.

"Story-book counseling" is a group guidance procedure which has been used effectively in at least one school (Anderson and Schmidt, 1967). This approach was used with first-, second-, and third-grade pupils. They met one-half hour every third week in relatively small groups. At these meetings, the counselor read stories describing children in different behavior situations. These stories were useful in encouraging discussions, and the pupils seemed to be able to identify with the characters in the stories. For the most part, the materials used in these classes were based on the work of Ojemann, Hawkins, and Chowing (1961) in *A Teaching Program in Human Relations and Mental Health.* In their description of the "story-book counseling" technique, Ojemann, *et al.,* (1961) refer to *Children and Books* by Arbuthnot (1957) as another source for locating appropriate story materials.

The "Unfinished Story" is a similar guidance technique which encourages discussion and provides situations suitable for role-playing. The authors have used unfinished stories with groups of pupils who were placed in remedial reading classes. For the most part, these pupils did not like school and did not participate in the cocurricular activities. These pupils seemed to be able to identify with the people in the unfinished stories and liked to discuss, write, or roleplay the possible solutions to the conflictual situation presented in the stories. In 1963, the *NEA Journal* began publishing "Unfinished Stories" that are appropriate for use with elementary-level pupils. These stories seem to be appropriate especially for guidance in personal and social relationships.

A sequential list of reading materials in the area of personal and social development has been published under the title of *Reading Ladders for Human Relations* (Crosby, 1963). According to the editor, "the books, in the ladder were chosen with the following purposes in mind: (1) to develop self-insight, (2) to create sensitivity to the experience of other individuals, (3) to develop expectations of differences among people, and (4) to extend insight into different value patterns" (p. 13). This reference is especially useful to the teacher since the books are graded according to age-level of the prospective reader, the books are annotated, and prices are given. In addition, the books are listed alphabetically and by themes.

Cole (1966) presents a very personal approach to the use of various art media in the classroom. She tells how to get the child to express himself in water colors, clay, story writing, dancing, and various other media. Cole's goal seems to be to free the child to be himself. She does this through establishing rapport by self-involvement and self-disclosure. She describes incidents from her own life and then uses these to stimulate the children to reveal their true feelings in whatever art media they are utilizing. Cole's method of using art for classroom involvement gives valuable clues to the group guidance specialist or classroom teacher for using art as a therapeutic media.

GROUP COUNSELING AND GROUP PLAY TECHNIQUES

A definition of group counseling has been given in chapter one of this text. This definition contains within it the assumption that group counselees are *basically normal individuals* with concerns not so debilitating as to require major personality modification. *Group counseling* has been the term applied to counseling of an *interview-type.* Few studies have been reported using *interview* group counseling with children below junior high school age. Ohlsen and Gazda (1965), however, obtained moderate success using primarily an interview-type of group counseling with fifth-grade underachievers. Their experience led them to recommend more use of roleplaying and play materials and smaller numbers in the group (five or six instead of eight to ten). Sonstegard (n.d.) used interview group counseling, following Adlerian counseling principles, with gifted underachievers in grades four to six. An informal evaluation suggested considerable positive change in the students' attitudes; however, Sonstegard also assisted the children's parents and teachers through group counseling.

Mercer (1958) describes an experience in multiple (group) counseling with sixth-grade children who were from a low-income housing area and who were selected because of their poor school attendance. The group was classroom-size and was referred to as an "Attendance Club," suggesting that it was closer to a guidance group than to a counseling group. Discussion techniques were employed. No control comparisons were available, but Mercer reported a general improvement in school attendance for the group participants.

Other than Adlerian interview methods applied to group counseling, which usually included counseling of parents and teachers also, few applications of interview group counseling used solely without play media have been reported. This is likely to be the result of the assumption (not clearly supported by research evidence) that discussion methods without the use of play media are *less* appropriate for children below junior high school age levels. Yet, *play therapy* seems an inappropriate term to be applied to designate the use of play media with *basically normal* children who receive group counseling help in the school setting. Play therapy may convey the presence of levels of disturbance in children that are considered beyond the scope of the school counselor. Many children with situational concerns can be helped by the school counselor through group counseling in a playroom setting with the use of play media, and it is recommended that the term *group play techniques* be substituted for *group play therapy* for use in these situations in the elementary school setting.

Sociodrama

Sociodrama utilized in the resolution of group problems also appears to offer much to the classroom teacher and the counselor in the elementary school. With the current interest in guidance and counseling in the elementary school, the guidance specialists will no doubt *rediscover* and thus revitalize this potent force for prevention and treatment of inter-personal problems. The use of the word rediscover is intentional and accurate. The following titles and dates indicate previous and current use of the technique: Gillies (1948) "Therapy Dramatics for the Public Schoolroom;" Haas (1949) *Psychodrama and Sociodrama in American Education;* and Jennings (1950) "Sociodrama as Educative Process." Barclay (1967), in a very recent study, utilized the sociodrama in conjunction with certain reinforcement techniques to improve the behavior of low status children in the elementary school classroom. Furthermore, the use of role-playing techniques (frequently synonymous with sociodrama) in assisting the elementary school child, is cited often in articles appearing in the newly found *Elementary School Guidance and Counseling* journal.

These two group procedures—group play techniques and sociodramatic techniques—endorsed by the authors, seem to offer the teachers and counselors the tools for working effectively with elementary school children. Thus, a definition of these techniques and a review of the relevant research is presented within this chapter along with the rationale for their use in the school setting.

Group Play Therapy

Slavson (1945, 1948) contends that there are three basic types of group therapy practiced, all with varying modifications: (1) play group therapy for young children (under twelve years of age); (2) activity group therapy for children in the latency period; and (3) interview group therapy for adolescents and adults. Strang (1958) also cites essentially the same three types of group therapy. The position taken by the authors of this chapter is in agreement with Slavson and Strang if the stipulation is added that the members of the treatment (therapy) groups are *not* within the normal behavioral range of their respective groups. For example, play group therapy would be Slavson's and Strang's preferred term to describe small group work with children not in the normal range of behavior, whereas the authors substitute group play techniques for small group work with children who have problems but are within the normal range of behavior for their age group.

The authors differentiate between guidance, counseling, and therapy to make certain issues more manifest—namely, that group psychotherapy should remain the province of those trained at the doctoral level in the various clinical fields of psychotherapy including, of course, psychiatry. This issue is presented here to discourage school personnel from counseling with seriously disturbed children. Nevertheless, when one considers the various processes of therapy that are currently practiced, save for psychopharmacological, electroshock, and surgical therapies, there is probably very little reason to insist that a therapist be required to receive training in medicine, or for that matter, at the doctoral level in other disciplines, though doctoral level training should provide the therapist with greater sophistication of techniques and, hopefully, with higher level ethical practices. In other words, there is no reason why most group play therapy techniques cannot be adapted for use by counselors in the school setting providing the group members are not seriously disturbed and that the counselor is trained in group counseling and play techniques and has the appropriate playroom facilities and play media available.

In order to understand and appreciate the value of group therapy, the reader should acquaint himself with play therapy used on a one-to-one basis, since it is from this form of treatment that many of the *group* play therapy techniques were developed. Selected references are included at the end of this chapter. Since space does not permit full treatment of group play therapy, the reader is referred to Ginott's (1961) *Group Psychotherapy with Children* and Ginott's (1968) "Group Therapy with Children" in *Basic Approaches to Group Psychotherapy and Group Counseling* for a more comprehensive treatment of the subject.

Klein (1955) assumes credit for the development of psychoanalytic play techniques in 1919. It is likely that play therapy was also first systematically described as a therapeutic procedure by Klein in 1919. However, Lebo (1955) credits Rousseau as the first to recommend that children be educated through play.

For a brief historical introduction of the educational and thera-peutic applications of play, see E. Liss's "Play Techniques in Child Analysis," *American Journal of Orthopsychiatry,* 1936. There have been a number of advocates and practitioners of play therapy in the United States. For a representative sampling of this work, the reader is referred to the suggested readings at the end of this chapter.

THEORETICAL RATIONALE AND VALUE
OF GROUP PLAY TECHNIQUES

Harms (1948) refers to play as "the language of childhood" (p. 237). Frank (1955) states that "in play we. . . observe various themes or schemes in which his [child's] immediate concerns are focused and more or less symbolically played out" (p. 585). Frank also refers to play as "learning to learn: . . . cope with life tasks," etc., (p. 583). It is generally agreed that all psychotherapy constitutes some form of learning. Axline (1955) succinctly conveys the authors' feeling on this issue in the following assertion regarding learning and psychotherapy: "It [psychotherapy] seems to be a cumulative, compound, in-tegrative, effective experience that can be used to illustrate many learning theories. At the same time, it raises many questions as to the adequacy of any existing theory to explain conclusively the learning experience that occurs during psychotherapy" (p. 622).[2]

In regard to therapeutic play, Conn (1951) states, "Every therapeutic play method is a form of learning process during which the child learns to accept and to utilize constructively that degree of personal responsibility and self-discipline neces-sary for effective self-expression and social living" (p. 753).

Lowrey (1955) contends that "We should be more accurate if we spoke of 'activity' [or activities] instead of 'play' with reference to therapy. For it is the activity with its release of fantasy, imagery, fears, hostility, and other feeling and thoughts

---

[2] From Axline, V. M.: Play therapy procedures and results. *American Journal of Orthopsychiatry,* 1955, *25,* 618-626. Copyright, the American Ortho-psychiatrist Association, Inc., reproduced by permission.

which give us quick insights into the problems besetting our child patients" (p. 574).[3]

Until now we have been speaking of play therapy without regard to its use in groups. What are the unique features or values that play in a group setting offer? Slavson (1945) claims that the function of the group in the treatment of young children lies in three areas: (1) play and activity; (2) association with other children of the same age; [and] (3) the role of the worker" (p. 208). The play and activity, according to Ginott (1961), should facilitate contact with the child, catharsis, insight, reality testing, and sublimation.

Slavson (1945) contends that in all instances the value of a group to children

> . . . lies in the fact it supplies a field in which the child may relate himself to others, thus helping him to break through isolation, withdrawal, and aggressive rejection of people . . . . to go out . . . into the human environment, thus leading from egocentricity and narcissism to object relationships . . . to test himself against others and discover the boundaries of his ego . . . [and] offers the possibility of developing patterns of relationship with human beings of the same intellectual, emotional, and social development, in which the feeling of sameness and therefore of comfort and security is greatest . . . (p. 209).[4]

The role of the group leader or "worker," according to Slavson (1945), varies with the age of the children; he is more active with the young child who is dependent upon him for support, and of necessity, for young children, much of the authority must come from the therapist. His role changes both with the ages of the children and with their changing personalities. "While he functions at first as a source of security and support, his role changes to one of guidance and authority" (p. 209).

Some specific values attached to play therapy are suggested by Solomon (1955). He contends that through

---

[3] From Lowrey, L. G.: Therapeutic play techniques: Introduction. *American Journal of Orthopsychiatry*, 1955, 25, 574-575. Copyright, the American Orthopsychiatric Association, Inc., reproduced by permission.

[4] From Slavson, S. R.: Differential methods of group therapy in relation to age levels. *Nervous Child*, 1945, 4, 196-210. Courtesy of the editor.

the use of play, the child is able to express his own regressive tendencies, thereby lessening the need to act out such forms of behavior in his real life situation . . . and the release of aggression or hostility with its appropriate emotion, that of anger, and the lessening of fears through the amelioration of the catastrophic results from the expression of the primitive impulses are well-established principles of gains which accrue from the judicious use of play therapy (p. 594).[5]

He summarizes the therapeutic value of play therapy as follows: "(1) release of hostility toward parents, siblings, etc.; (2) alleviation of guilt feelings; (3) opportunity to express freely all love fantasies; (4) incorporation of therapeutic suggestions in direction of growth; and (5) desensitization by means of repetition" (Solomon, 1940, p. 763).[6]

On the other side of the ledger, Bender (1955) wrote, "If the play technique used is important to the adult and gives him a tool with which he can understand the child and relate to him with confidence and warmth, the play setup will undoubtedly contribute to the relationship. Beyond this I doubt if there is any specific therapeutic value to the play procedures" (p. 785).[7]

Sociodrama and Psychodrama

J. L. Moreno (1944), the father of the sociodrama and psychodrama, has defined sociodrama as "a deep action method dealing with inter-group relations and collective ideologies"; whereas he defined psychodrama as "a deep action method dealing with interpersonal relations and private ideologies" (p. 3). Moreno contends that "sociodrama has two roots—socius which means the associate, the other fellow, and drama, which means

---

[5] From Solomon, J. C.: Play techniques and the integrative process. *American Journal of Orthopsychiatry*, 1955, *25*, 591-600. Copyright, the American Orthopsychiatric Association, Inc., reproduced by permission.

[6] From Solomon, J. C.: Active play therapy: Further experiences. *American Journal of Orthopsychiatry*, 1940, *10*, 763-781. Copyright, the American Orthopsychiatric Association, Inc., reproduced by permission.

[7] From Bender, L.: Therapeutic play techniques: Discussion. *American Journal of Orthopsychiatry*, 1955, *25*, 784-787. Copyright, the American Orthopsychiatric Association, Inc., reproduced by permission.

action. Sociodrama would mean action in behalf of the other fellow" (p. 3).

The concept underlying the sociodramatic approach is that *"man is a role-player"* (Moreno, 1944, p. 5). Furthermore, every role has two sides, a private and a collective side. The roles which are characterized by collective ideas and experiences are sociodramatic roles, and those characterized by individual ideas and experiences are psychodramatic roles (Moreno, 1944).

To delineate further Moreno's intended meaning of the sociodrama, once more the reader is directed to Moreno's own description of the sociodrama. He believes the true subject of the sociodrama to be the group—the group being as large as the culture and organized by the social and cultural roles. In other words, the group in sociodrama corresponds to the individual in psychodrama, but because the group is only a metaphor and its existence is composed of the inter-related individuals representative of the same culture, the individuals as representatives of the culture and not their private selves become the subjects of the action (Moreno, 1944). Another way of describing the sociodrama is that it concerns one's difficulties with another person. The participants in the drama represent character types rather than themselves. (The nature of the "type," however, must be projected by the individual actor and portray much of the character of the actor.)

Corsini (1966) defines sociodrama as "roleplaying which focuses on the problem of the group" (p. 201). And, "if. . . a problem is acted out in a group and has meaning to all the members, the procedure is known as sociodrama" (p. 87). By contrast, Corsini defines psychodrama as "role-playing by a person of his own past, present, or future situation" (p. 200). "Psychodrama occurs when an individual acts out his own problem" (p. 87). Corsini emphasizes that roleplaying is a part of both psychodrama and sociodrama. He contends that roleplaying is the inclusive term for spontaneity action techniques.

From the above definitions, one can conclude that the psychodrama is a more personal form of therapy than the sociodrama, i.e., the object of the treatment is the person himself rather than a symbol of persons or roles as represented through the socio-drama. Also, roleplaying is used in both sociodrama and psycho-drama and is an action technique without regard to emphasis—personal or social, individual or group.

In actual practice, the three terms—sociodrama, psychodrama, and roleplaying—are frequently used interchangeably and the individual roleplaying a social or group problem frequently projects his own problems through the role and attempts to work through the problem for himself as well as for improved group understanding.

Research of Socio- and Psychodramatic Technique. As early as 1941, Alpert (1941) described a teacher's application of "spontaneous dramatizations" and group therapy discussions to kindergarten children suffering from an unwholesome use of scatological language. Alpert reported that the treatment led to a decrease in the use of scatological language and that the "educational group therapy," in addition to the removal of the symptom, helped free the children from guilt and anxiety through the teacher's interpretations and universalizing of the symptom which permitted the children to abreact it in their play and obtain relief and release.

Gillies (1948) reported the successful application of "therapy dramatics" in drawing out and involving normal first-grade children of six and seven years of age. To stimulate dramatiza-tion, Gillies started the groups with simple nursery rhymes, such as "There was a Crooked Man," and "Sing a Song of Six-pence." This was followed with appropriate stories, such as, *Daddies: What They Do All Day* by Helen Walker Puner, and piano music or self-devised rhythm bands.

Brunelle (1949) utilized a literary source book: *Reading Ladders for Human Relations* published by the American Council on Education, to select objective *conflict* situations in human relations to be roleplayed in the elementary school classrooms. After reading a given conflict situation, selection of roleplayers was made by the classroom teacher, and the session was role-played, discussed, and replayed until the students and teacher were satisfied with the handling of the conflict situation. Brunelle concluded, "Research indicates that there is considerable carry-over from the training situations to real life situations when roleplaying is used. It is this *carry over* that makes role playing such a significant educational technique" (p. 237).

Roleplaying or psychodrama, later called the spontaneity approach to creative teaching, was used successfully by Cole (1949) to desensitize fifth graders to rebuff and discouragement.

Shaftel and Shaftel (1949) reported introducing sociodramas into fifth-, sixth-, and seventh-grade classrooms through the use of problem stories written especially for the purpose of warm up. "These problem stories were based upon the developmental tasks of middle childhood and critical situations as found in literature of child development . . . each story was structured to bring its problem to a climax, but not to solve its dilemma" (p. 246).

Teachers in the elementary schools of Inglewood, California utilized sociodrama developed around vocational, travel, family conflict, and classroom conflict topics to "explore key children in action," and discovered that former uncooperative children frequently gave good sociodramatic performances, and that insights pass between pupil and pupil and between pupil and teacher. The teachers discovered "how problems of human relations could be resolved openly through group enactment and evaluation as well as how social skills could be built, through spontaneity practice, by children who needed them" (Haas, 1949, p. 262).

Wells (1962), a school administrator, cites her successful application of roleplaying counseling (psychodrama) in the elementary school. She used a variety of the psychodrama situations which included on the spot, future enactment, and "here and now," with children from first to eighth grade. She also utilized role reversal, double ego, soliloquy, and conscience in the roleplaying. Usually the group psychodramas consisted of only two or three children, sometimes a teacher or parent, and the director (Cecilia Wells). The problems of these normal children included, "quarrels over possessions, rivalry for position in a game or line, tripping or hitting each other—especially on the playground, interference with each other's classroom activities, classroom behavior unacceptable for the learning situation, and academic inadequacies" (p. 244).

Boyd and Youssi (1958) used five open-ended problem stories dealing with home situations, school incidents, and the school community to learn more about the attitudes and values of class members, and to study the reactions of the class toward individual members. They recommend that the elementary school teachers use these procedures as a diagnostic technique and to improve understanding of the values, attitudes, maturity, etc., of their students.

Based on the results of a pilot study of the use of sociodrama by classroom teachers, Shaftel and Shaftel (1949) succintly describe why the sociodrama is recommended for classroom teacher's use in the elementary school:

> (1) sociodrama is a helpful elementary school teaching device that can be *adequately* used by inexperienced and relatively unskilled teachers, and very *effectively* used by master teachers, if appropriate dramatic "warm-up" materials are provided for initial sessions; (2) enables the teacher to explore attitudes of her pupils in areas which do not usually enter classroom experiences (home and neighborhood life, for example) as a basis for further learning; (3) it fosters a permissive atmosphere in which pupils feel free to express their own feelings and attitudes for more socially acceptable generalizations; (4) it gives pupils an opportunity to express solutions in terms of their own drives and impulses which are often on a different level from their verbalizations (p. 252).[8]

In addition to the utility of the sociodrama as suggested above, Moreno's theoretical rationale emphasizes the value of *spontaneity* and the resultant catharsis assisting a person to encounter new situations with flexibility, confidence, and accuracy.

Corsini (1966) lists simultaneity (creation of total involvement), spontaneity (learning while in a situation devoid of threat), and veridicality (approximation of reality situation) as

----

[8] From Shaftel, G., and Shaftel, F. R.: Report on the use of a "practice action level" in the Stanford University project for American Ideals. In R. B. Haas (Ed.): *Psychodrama and Sociodrama in American Education*, 1949. Courtesy of Beacon House, Inc., Beacon, New York.

unique values of roleplaying (his inclusive term including both sociodrama and psychodrama).

Based on the concept of developmental tasks, the classroom teacher or sociodrama leader can select those tasks of a social nature which a child must learn and assign the task or theme to the group for dramatization, and through a system of reinforcing acceptable behavior, condition the group to the mores of the culture or subculture. Barclay (1967), in a recent study, cites the successful application of reinforcement techniques through sociodrama and other means with low status fifth graders.

The reported research in the application of sociodramatic and psychodramatic techniques is representative of the studies which have been conducted in this field. These are, of course, primarily clinical rather than experimental with appropriate controls, and it is obvious that more rigorous research must be done before we are in a position to endorse these methods without some reservations. They do, nevertheless, represent the authors' preference for treating, through action methods, the elementary school child in a group.

Assuming that all forms of guidance and counseling are based on the concepts of learning or unlearning and relearning, there is evidence to suggest that action techniques such as the sociodrama, psychodrama, and roleplaying are especially adaptable to behavior therapy and reinforcement techniques.

THEORETICAL FRAMEWORK—ROLEPLAYING AND BEHAVIOR THEORY

An attempt will be made below to develop, for purposes of use in the elementary school, a rapprochement between action techniques of sociodrama and psychodrama (roleplaying) and learning theory models applied in counseling and therapy. For purposes of economy, sociodrama and psychodrama will be considered to be essentially the same—the chief difference being one of emphasis on an individual problem in the psychodrama as compared with a group problem in the case of sociodrama. Both sociodrama and psychodrama are forms of roleplaying—the overarching concept.

Basic Assumptions

Certain basic assumptions are outlined below which suggest that the roleplaying techniques of sociodrama and psychodrama are especially applicable for use with the elementary school child.

1. "Actions speak louder than words" for most young children. Young children, by nature, enjoy roleplaying and utilize it for much of their problem solving.

2. Playing a role permits the young child to experience himself in action—confrontation with himself and others in the group in a problem solving situation, while at the same time the role provides him with the security, if he needs it, of make-believe.

3. Roleplaying includes thinking, acting, and feeling which are heightened by their interaction creating a total involvement (Corsini, 1966).

4. The young child requires more structure than adults in his personal and/or social problem solving. Roleplaying permits the child to isolate the problem areas and attack the defined problem or use the roleplaying setting to isolate the problem.

5. The child has a strong need to be accepted both by his peer group and adults. (Both situations are possible in the sociodrama and group psychodrama—the peers composing the group and the adult, the teacher or counselor who leads the group.)

Steps in Sociodrama and Psychodrama

There are certain procedures that are common to both sociodrama and psychodrama and others that are pertinent to only one or the other. Below a comparison is made based on the basic aspects of each technique. Jennings (1950) has tested the steps of the sociodrama and Sturm (1965) has listed what he refers to as "six of the more important psychodramatic techniques" (p. 52).

SOCIODRAMA	PSYCHODRAMA
The main steps in sociodrama are, according to Jennings, (1950, p. 264):	The main techniques (in order of use) of psychodrama are, according to Sturm, (1965, pp. 52-57):
1. Volunteering of participants;	1. Warm-up;
2. The warming up of participants;	2. Problem-presentation (Consensus is reached regarding which problem is to be the focus for a particular session.);

SOCIODRAMA	PSYCHODRAMA
3. Free ventilation of feeling and reaction of group members and the players,	3. Self-presentation (The subject describes the setting and enacts or describes those involved in the problem.);
4. Analysis by group members and players, and	4. Role-playing (Problem is roleplayed utilizing the many variations including auxiliary egos.);
5. Summary and recommendation by group members.	5. Catharsis; and
	6. Group participation.

In addition to the five steps cited above, Jennings (1950) also cautions the teacher who uses and directs the sociodrama that (1) the situation must be *representative* of the problems of group members; (2) the majority of the group members must want to explore the situation; and (3) the teacher should be willing to have the problem explored (p. 263).

Close scrutiny of the steps and techniques in the sociodrama and psychodrama reveals that they are very much alike. Jennings and Sturm used different phraseology but, essentially, both techniques include the use of the concept of *readiness* which is generated by various *warm up* techniques; both techniques encourage catharsis and openness through spontaneous ventilation of feelings and beliefs; both techniques are roleplaying (in the Corsini sense) and utilize various manifestations of dramatization; both techniques utilize group involvement; and though not listed as a step or technique, both include the possibility for replaying part or all of the drama. The basic difference between sociodrama and psychodrama is the greater degree of emphasis in psychodrama on the personal problems of the individuals as contrasted with the social nature of the problems for the group in sociodrama.

Comparison of Roleplaying (Sociodrama and Psychodrama) With A Behavioristically-Oriented Approach to Group Counseling and Therapy

On various occasions Moreno (1949, 1963) has referred to the similarities between sociodrama and psychodrama and learning theory approaches to psychotherapy. Recently Sturm (1965) has described the similarities between psychodrama and behavioristically-oriented therapies. A behavior therapist, well known for his application of behavioral or learning principles to *group* therapy, Arnold Lazarus (1968), has stated that "there is nothing in modern learning theory to justify withholding the combined advantages of interpretation and desensitization, or any other method or technique which seems to have beneficial effects" (p. 155). Sturm (1965) asserts that "the basic principles underlying psychodrama can be seen to be like those of behavior therapy and indeed of all psychotherapy. . ." (p. 57). Gazda (1968) has also attempted a rapprochement between learning theory principles and conditions found essential to behavioral modification in a group setting. His basic premise is that attitude and behavioral modification resulting from a therapeutic relationship must be explained through *learning* concepts and principles, and that various types of learning may account for changes which occur because of the application of various therapy and counseling techniques. The concept of two-factor learning has been introduced by Mowrer (1960), and it is quite feasible that we have multifactor learning which might account for the success of many different therapeutic approaches. The following table represents an attempt at still another rapproachement—between sociodrama and psychodrama and behavioristically-oriented therapies.

SOCIODRAMA AND PSYCHODRAMA	BEHAVIORISTICALLY-ORIENTED THERAPIES
1. Warm-up readiness): Here the attempt is made to decrease the clients' fears and to encourage openness and spontaneity through physical touching, smiling, and pleasant talk including introductions and sometimes a description or clarification of client expectations prior to actual assumption of roles and the introduction of the clients' problems.	1. Systematic desensitization: The clients are encouraged to relax through physiological means and the general demeanor of the therapist in *preparation* for the introduction of mild anxiety into the relationship.
2. Catharsis through spontaneity: Here Moreno (1944) differentiates between catharsis in the sociodrama and psychodrama. Essentially, however, he intends the catharsis to evoke a positive feeling leading to *integration.* "A catharsis of integration is constituted by an increased action insight and greater ability for self-restraint and flexibility as the situation demands" (Moreno and Kipper, 1968, p. 59).	2. Reciprocal inhibition: Certain behavioral therapists encourage clients to make responses incompatible with anxiety including, among others, sexual responses, relaxation, assertiveness, eating, and the like.
3. Action through the socio- and psychodrama (roleplaying): Roleplay-	3. It is feasible that most if not all versions of the behavioral therapists

SOCIODRAMA AND PSYCHODRAMA

ing or dramatization is the essence of socio- and psychodrama, or as Corsini (1966) puts it, "The patient operates holistically, not partially" (pp. 12-13). The experiencing by the actor (protagonist) and the analysis by the director and group members constitute a system of rewards and punishment of the nature of operant conditioning, shaping, reciprocal inhibition, systematic desensitization, assertive training, emotive imagery, and still other versions of behavioristically-oriented therapies. Haas (1949) describes the use of roleplaying (psychodrama) to desensitize fifth graders to the fear of going from house to house soliciting papers for a paper drive, and Jennings (1950) states, "Any situations which hold a destructive emotional impact for most members of a given minority group require classroom exploration [sociodrama] to densensitize the individuals toward that experience, as much as to foster their cultivation of skills with which to face it" (p. 276).

4. Group involvement: The group helps create a microcosm of the larger society and this creates a milieu for reality testing and also it provides a tremendous therapeutic lift through its peer support (reinforcement) of each client.

5. Role-repetition or modifications of roleplaying, e.g., doubling, mirror, and role-reversal techniques, provide the protagonist(s) with the opportunity for reexperiencing a situation or event.

BEHAVIORISTICALLY-ORIENTED
THERAPIES

utilize one or more types of roleplaying since their emphasis is on the change of *overt* behavior, e.g., symptom modification and/or motoric modification through operant conditioning, etc. Bandura and Walters (1963) suggest support for the assumption that there is a close relationship and/or utility between sociodrama (at least) and principles of conditioning when they stated, "Should one wish to produce discriminative social learning, the best procedure would undoubtedly be set up actual or symbolic social situations and repeatedly reward desired responses to these stimuli, while punishing undesirable responses or letting these go unrewarded" (p. 248).

Bandura (1965) and Lazarus (1968) also describe the use of roleplaying in assertive training, and Sturm (1965) states ". . . it appears that anxiety can be reciprocally inhibited within the psychodramatic technique of *roleplaying* . . ." (p. 59).

4. According to Lazarus (1968), "Generally speaking, in desensitization groups, therapy takes place primarily *in* but not *by* the group. . . . However, this is not true for assertive training groups. Here, the role of the therapist usually evolves from that of instructor to a participant observer" (p. 161). In assertive training groups, peer group support (reinforcement) is a very therapeutic element in change just as it is in sociodrama and psychodrama.

Aside from the use of the group for reinforcement purposes, learning principles would support the probability of the group maximizing response and stimulus generalization.

5. Role-repetition creates conditions which would appear especially appropriate for the application of shaping, also appropriate for discriminate training, assertive training, emotive imagery, and possibly even the broader concepts of operant conditioning, systematic desensitization, and reciprocal inhibition.

In other words the possibility of replaying a role several times gives the group leader and group members the opportunity to reinforce and shape appropriate behavior and ignore or punish inappropriate behavior in various patterns and/or sequences as illustrated by the learning principles cited above.

The foregoing comparison between action methods (sociodrama and psychodrama or roleplaying) of therapeutic group approaches and learning concepts or principles of behavioristically-oriented approaches to therapy, is admittedly a forced one at the moment. However, there appears to be enough similarity and common elements present to warrant closer scrutiny through a systematic application of learning principles in conjunction with action-oriented group approaches to therapy such as Barclay's (1967) use of sociodrama with certain reinforcement techniques to improve the behavior of low-status children in the elementary school. In other words, action techniques such as sociodrama, psychodrama, and play techniques show promise of being explained by means of the laws of learning and certain learning-related principles of behavior therapy. This would enhance the principles of behavior therapy and action techniques in their growth toward becoming a science.

QUALIFICATIONS OF GROUP LEADERS

The leaders who have reported successful application of group procedures (from group guidance to play therapy) have ranged from regular classroom teachers who were untrained in group techniques to psychologists and psychiatrists who were highly trained in group therapy. When the emphasis is chiefly providing information in a group with an indirect purpose of changing attitudes and behavior (as in group guidance), the group leader should be competent as an instructor and possess an understanding of group process or dynamics; however, as the aim or intent of the group procedure moves from instruction to counseling to therapy, greater understanding is required of group therapeutic procedures, and the leader must possess the certification or licensing required for his professional role.

Unfortunately, qualification for group procedures (namely counseling, therapy, and play techniques) have not been clearly defined. A creative teacher who understands group process can successfully perform group guidance functions, and some can successfully utilize sociodramatic and even psychodramatic techniques. Generally speaking, however, the latter two techniques have been used more successfully by teachers under the supervision of a trained socio- or psychodramatist.

The editor (Gazda, 1968) has described the qualifications of a group counselor in some detail in his chapter, "A Functional Approach to Group Counseling," in *Basic Approaches to Group Psychotherapy and Group Counseling.* He contends that group counseling comes *after* expertise in individual counseling and thus usually in the second year of graduate training, during which time courses in group guidance and/or group dynamics, group counseling, and practicum in group counseling are taken. For the group counselor in the elementary school, play techniques should be included in the theory and methods courses and applied in practicum.

The seriously disturbed child does not usually receive his primary treatment in the public school setting; therefore unless the school is fortunate enough to have the services of doctoral-level child specialists (sociological, psychological, or psychiatric), most group psychotherapy will not be done in the school setting. However, with the disturbed child who, for the most part, is able to remain in the classroom, group therapy procedures—sociodrama, psychodrama, and play techniques—are recommended as suitable when performed by a counselor trained in these procedures who is also under the supervision of a psychiatrist.

SELECTION OF GROUP MEMBERS

Group Guidance

Group guidance is applicable to all students enrolled in preschool classes through high school. In the preschool and elementary school classes, such group guidance techniques as puppet shows, "unfinished stories," "story book counseling," the use of movies, and art media are appropriate to all the students in a particular class since the aim is prevention of problem behavior through instructing the group in such guidance related goals as fair play, taking turns, sharing and how to listen. As a rule, the entire class participates in a group guidance session; however, there may be occasions when the teacher or group leader will utilize sociodramatic or roleplaying techniques with only a few individuals involved in a conflict. The selection for the socio-drama may involve the contesting parties and/or volunteers who represent them.

Group Counseling and Group Play Techniques

Since group counseling for the age group five to eleven generally involves the application of play media and techniques, the suggestions which follow for selection of group members will pertain to the more global area of group play techniques.

1. Slavson (1943) and Ginott (1968) both consider the basic prerequisite for admission to a therapy group the presence of or the capacity for *social hunger* within the child. The authors of this chapter are in agreement with the intent of this principle, but in actual practice it is difficult to exclude children who have a minimum of social hunger unless their behavior is grossly anti-social and usually these children are also excluded from the school setting.

2. The concept of role balancing is suggested as a general rule of thumb to follow. This means that one should avoid overloading a group with a particular behavioral type, such as aggressive, hyperactive children, but rather include one hyperactive child with a withdrawn child or two and one or two with dissimilar syndromes. Or, as Ginott (1968) states, "An effeminate boy needs to identify with more masculine playmates. The dependent child needs the example of more self-reliant groupmates. . . .Aggressive youngsters need group-mates who are strong but not belligerent. Fearful children need to be placed in a group of more mature youngsters" (p. 177).

3. Age and sex constitute two additional categories that one must consider in composing groups for treatment by play techniques or group counseling. Ginott (1968) recommends that preschool children are appropriately placed in mixed sex groups, whereas school-age children should be separated by sexes. The authors of this chapter agree in part with Ginott; however, they have found mixed sex groups to be therapy engendering up to preadolescence or at approximately

age ten or eleven at which point the sexual aggressiveness of the girls, who are more mature than the boys at this age, interferes with the therapy rather than promotes it.

For the most part, children of the same age constitute the most therapeutic grouping. Exceptions are made deliberately to place more aggresive children in older aged groups and immature children in younger age groups. Ginott (1968) recommends that groupmates should not differ in age by more than twelve months other than for the exceptions cited above.

4. Differences in ethnic backgrounds, race, and intelligence are not serious handicaps for young children to rise above unless there are, for example, gross differences in intelligence, e.g., the retarded grouped with those of average intellectual ability or better.

GROUP SIZE

Guidance groups, by nature of their purpose or design, are or may be equivalent to a regular size class of approximately fifteen to thirty-five. These groups may be larger than counseling or play therapy groups because the goals are different, i.e., basically teaching or imparting of information pertinent to developing healthy attitudes and behavior versus a *direct* attempt in group counseling or play group techniques to modify attitudes and behavior by encouraging the expression of feelings, actions, fears, beliefs, etc., for the purpose of understanding their appropriateness or inappropriateness for the child.

Counseling and play group therapy or techniques, therefore, are much smaller than guidance groups. The range is from two to six or seven. With the more hyperactive children, those in need of more structure and control, two to five is the preferred number. With the passive or withdrawing in the majority, six or seven may be worked with simultaneously. The counselor should remember that each time he adds an additional child to his group he loses a certain degree of control; it is necessary that the group counselor or play group therapist be in control of his group. The editor of this volume has described elsewhere (Gazda, 1968) the concept of *preliminary* or *trial grouping* as a means of selecting the most therapeutic or facilitative group.

Basically, trial grouping means that more children than the preferred number for a group are placed in a group for three or four sessions and then the best combinations or mutually therapeutic members are placed in respective groups. This method is, of course, applicable only to closed groups. Open groups may be organized by means of trial groupings, but new members will be added as role openings occur through termination of certain children.

DURATION OF TREATMENT

Guidance groups continue throughout the child's school career. The goals are modified in accordance with the developmental tasks and critical incidents (see Gazda and Folds, 1968) of the maturing child.

The duration of counseling and play therapy or play technique groups varies with the degree of behavior modification required and the frequency of sessions. As a general principle or rule, one develops greater intensity of treatment the more frequently a group meets. Some children during crises may require daily meetings of forty to sixty minutes versus the norm for most groups of one or two (equally spaced) one-hour meetings a week. The school counselor will have to gauge the frequency of group meetings in terms of the time of year and numbers of weeks remaining in the school year. Near the beginning of a school year, once-a-week meetings may be appropriate; whereas near the latter part of the year, more frequent meetings would be required to reach optimum intensity or therapeutic effectiveness for group members. Also, preventive treatment will likely be shorter in duration than remedial treatment.

SUMMARY

This chapter outlines the application of large group (group guidance) and small group (group counseling and group play techniques) procedures in the elementary school—including preschool children and the child up to the age of ten or eleven.

The emphasis is on the preventative application of group procedures within the elementary school setting including group guidance techniques utilized by the teacher and group counseling and play group techniques used by the counselor. The counselor is described as functioning in the tripartite role of counseling, consultation, and coordination within the elementary school.

The concept of developmental task is described as the counselor's and teacher's benchmark for gauging the adequacy of a child's coping behavior and hence his counseling and guidance needs.

Group counseling is defined for the early elementary school child as basically an action technique employing sociodramatic and psychodramatic principles. These sociodrama and psychodrama tenents are compared with learning theory and/or behavioral counseling and therapy concepts and principles. The comparison reveals a high degree of similarity between them. The purpose of this comparison is to show that these group action techniques are more than an art, i.e., they also have within them the elements of a science.

The chapter closes with a description of the qualifications of a group counselor for his role in the elementary school; it outlines the procedure for selecting and grouping of children for group guidance, group counseling, and play group techniques; gives the preferred size of groups; and the frequency and duration of treatment is detailed.

A list of selected readings in group guidance, group counseling, sociodrama, psychodrama, and group play therapy is provided at the end of the chapter for the reader who wishes to study these procedures in greater depth.

REFERENCES

Alpert, A.: Education as therapy. *Psychoanalytic Quarterly,* 1941, *10,* 468-474.

Anderson, J., and Schmidt, W. I.: A time for feeling. *Elementary School Guidance and Counseling,* 1967, *1,* 47-56.

Arbuthnot, M.: *Children and Books.* Chicago: Scott, Foresman, 1957.

Axline, V. M.: Play therapy procedures and results. *American Journal of Orthopsychiatry,* 1955, *25,* 618-626.

Bandura, A.: Behavioral modification through modeling procedures. In L.

Krasner and L. P. Ullmann (Eds.): *Research in Behavior Modification.* New York: Holt, Rinehart & Winston, 1965. pp. 310-340.

Bandura, A., and Walters, R. H.: *Social Learning and Personality Development.* New York: Holt, 1963.

Barclay, J. R.: Effecting behavior change in the elementary classroom: An exploratory study. *Journal of Counseling Psychology,* 1967, *14,* 240-247.

Bender, L.: Therapeutic play techniques: Discussion. *American Journal of Orthopsychiatry,* 1955, *25,* 784-787.

Bender, L., and Woltmann, A. G.: The use of puppet shows as a psychotherapeutic method for behavior problems in children. *American Journal of Orthopsychiatry,* 1936, *6,* 341-354.

Blocher, D. H.: *Developmental Counseling.* New York: Ronald, 1966.

Boyd, A., and Youssi, M.: Peer group regulates role playing. *School Counselor,* 1958, *6,* 11-18.

Brammer, L. M., and Shostrom, E. L.: *Therapeutic Psychology,* Englewood Cliffs, New Jersey: Prentice-Hall, 1960.

Brunelle, P.: Action projects from children's literature; An indirect approach to intercultural relations in the elementary school. In R. B. Haas (Ed.): *Psychodrama and Sociodrama in American Education.* Beacon, New York: Beacon House, 1949. pp. 235-242.

Cole, N.: *Children's Arts From Deep Down Inside.* New York: John Day, 1966.

Cole, N. R.: Exploring psychodrama at fifth grade level. In R. B. Haas (Ed.): *Psychodrama and Sociodrama in American Education.* New York: Beacon House, 1949. pp. 243-245.

Conn, J. H.: Play interview therapy of castration fears. *American Journal of Orthopsychiatry,* 1955, *25,* 747-754.

Corsini, R. J.: *Roleplaying in Psychotherapy.* Chicago: Aldine, 1966.

Crosby, M. (Ed.): *Reading Ladders for Human Relations* (4th ed.) Washington, D. C.: American Council on Education, 1963.

Davis, C. D.: A group technique for the modification of certain behavior reactions (kindergarten level). (Doctoral dissertation, State University of Iowa) Ann Arbor, Mich.: University Microfilms, 1958. No. 57-1608.

Denney, E. W.: A study of the effectiveness of selected motion pictures for reducing frustration in children. *Dissertation Abstracts,* 1959, *19,* 3170-3171.

Erickson, E. H.: *Childhood and Society.* New York: W. W. Norton, 1950.

Frank, L. K.: Play in personality development. *American Journal of Orthopsychiatry,* 1955, *25,* 576-590.

Gazda, G. M.: A functional approach to group counseling. In G. M. Gazda (Ed.): *Basic Approaches to Group Psychotherapy and Group Counseling.* Springfield, Ill.: Charles C Thomas, 1968. pp. 263-303.

Gazda, G. M., and Ohlsen, M. M.: Group counseling—A means of parent education. *Adult Leadership,* 1966, *14,* 231 ff.

Gazda, G. M., and Folds, J. H.: *Group Guidance: A Critical Incidents Approach.* Chicago: Follett, 1968.

Gessell, A., and Ilg, F.: *The Child from Five to Ten,* New York: Harper, 1946.

Gillies, E. P.: Therapy dramatics for public schoolroom. *Nervous Child,* 1948, *17,* 328-336.

Ginott, H. G.: *Group Psychotherapy with Children: The Theory and Practice of Play Therapy.* New York: McGraw-Hill, 1961.

Ginott, H. G.: Group therapy with Children. In G. M. Gazda (Ed.): *Basic Approaches to Group Psychotherapy and Group Counseling,* Springfield, Ill.: Charles C Thomas, 1968. pp. 176-194.

Goldman, L.: Group guidance: Content and process. *Personnel and Guidance Journal,* 1962, *40,* 518-522.

Haas, R. B. (Ed.): *Psychodrama and Sociodrama in American Education.* New York: Beacon House, 1949.

Harms, E.: Play diagnosis: Preliminary considerations for a sound approach. *Nervous Child,* 1948, 7, 233-246.

Havighurst, R. J.: *Developmental Tasks and Education.* Chicago: University of Chicago Press, 1948.

Havighurst, R. J.: *Human Development and Education.* New York: David McKay, 1953.

Hill, G. E.: Agreements in the practice of guidance in the elementary schools. *Elementary School Guidance and Counseling,* 1967, *1,* 188-195.

Jennings, H. H.: Sociodrama as an educative process. In *Fostering Mental Health in Our Schools.* Washington, D. C.: Association for Supervision and Curriculum Development, N.E.A., 1950. pp. 260-285.

Klein, M.: The psychoanalytic play technique. *American Journal of Orthopsychiatry,* 1955, *25,* 223-237.

Lazarus, A.: Behavior therapy in groups. In G. M. Gazda (Ed.): *Basic Approaches to Group Psychotherapy and Group Counseling.* Springfield, Ill.: Charles C Thomas, 1968. pp. 149-175.

Lebo, D.: The development of play as a form of therapy. *American Journal of Psychiatry,* 1955, *12,* 418-442.

Levy, D. M.: Psychotherapy and childhood. *American Journal of Psychotherapy,* 1940, *10,* 905-910.

Lilienthal, J. W., III, and Tryon, C.: Developmental tasks: II. Discussion of specific tasks and implications. In *Fostering Mental Health in Our Schools.* Washington, D. C.: Association for Supervision and Curriculum Development, N.E.A., 1950. pp. 90-128.

Liss, E.: Play techniques in child analysis. *American Journal of Orthopsychiatry,* 1936, *6,* 17-22.

Lowrey, L. G.: Therapeutic play techniques: Introduction. *American Journal of Orthopsychiatry,* 1955. *25,* 574-575.

Meeks, A.: Dimensions of elementary school guidance. *Elementary School Guidance and Counseling.* 1967, *1,* 163-187.

Mercer, B. W.: Multiple counseling at the elementary school level. *School Counselor,* 1958, *6,* 12-14.

Moreno, J. L.: Sociodrama: A method for the analysis of social conflicts. *Psychodrama Monographs,* 1944, No. 1.

Moreno, J. L.: The spontaneity theory of learning. In R. B. Haas (Ed.): *Psychodrama and Sociodrama in American Education.* Beacon, New York: Beacon House, 1949. pp. 191-197.

Moreno, J. L.: Behaviour therapy. *American Journal of Psychiatry,* 1963, *120,* 194-196.

Moreno, J. L., and Kipper, D. A.: Group psychodrama and community-centered counseling. In G. M. Gazda (Ed.): *Basic Approaches to Group Psychotherapy and Group Counseling.* Springfield, Ill.: Charles C Thomas, 1968. pp. 27-79.

Mowrer, O. H.: *Learning Theory and Behavior.* New York: Wiley, 1960.

Ohlsen, M. M., and Gazda, G. M.: Counseling underachieving bright students. *Education,* 1965, *86,* 78-81.

Ojemann, R. H.; Hawkins, A., and Chowing, K.: *A Teaching Program in Human Behavior and Mental Health.* Iowa City, Iowa: University of Iowa Press, 1961.

Patterson, C. H.: Elementary school counselor or child development specialist? *Personnel and Guidance Journal,* 1967, *46,* 75-76.

Shaftel, G., and Shaftel, F. R.: Report on the use of a "practice action level" in the Stanford University project for American ideals. In R. B. Haas (Ed.): *Psychodrama and Sociodrama in American Education.* New York: Beacon House, 1949. pp. 245-253.

Slavson, S. R.: *An Introduction to Group Therapy.* New York: The Commonwealth Fund and International Universities Press, 1943.

Slavson, S. R.: Differential methods of group therapy in relation to age levels. *Nervous Child,* 1945, *4,* 196-210.

Slavson, S. R.: Group therapy in child care and child guidance. *Jewish Social Service Quarterly,* 1948, *25,* 203-213.

Solomon, J. C.: Active play therapy: Further experiences. *American Journal of Orthopsychiatry,* 1940, *10,* 763-781.

Solomon, J. C.: Play techniques and the integrative process. *American Journal of Orthopsychiatry,* 1955, *25,* 591-600.

Sonstegard, M. S.: A demonstration of group counseling procedures to help low-producing talented and gifted pupils in the elementary school. Quincy, Ill.: Quincy Public Schools, n.d.

Strang, R.: *Group Work in Education.* New York: Harper, 1958.

Sturm, I. E.: The behavioristic aspect of psychodrama. *Group Psychotherapy,* 1965, *18,* 50-64.

Tryon, C., and Lilienthal, J. W., III: Developmental tasks: I. The concept and its importance. In *Fostering Mental Health in Our Schools.* Washington, D. C.: Association for Supervision and Curriculum Development, N.E.A., 1950. pp. 77-89.

Wells, C. G.: Psychodrama and creative counseling in the elementary school. *Group Psychotherapy*, 1962, *15*, 244-252.

Zaccaria, J.: Developmental tasks: Implications for the goals of guidance. *Personnel and Guidance Journal*, 1965, *44*, 372-375.

SUGGESTED READING

Axline, V. M.: Non-directive therapy for poor readers. *Journal of Counseling Psychology*, 1947, *2*, 61-69.

Baruch, D. W.: Therapeutic procedures as a part of the educative process. *Journal of Counseling Psychology*, 1940, *4*, 165-172.

Baruch, D. W.: Incorporation of therapeutic procedures as part of the educative process: A further report. *American Journal of Orthopsychiatry*, 1942, *12*, 659-665.

Beiser, H. R.: Play equipment for diagnosis and therapy. *American Journal of Orthopsychiatry*, 1955, *25*, 761-770.

Bender, L., and Woltman, A. G.: The use of plastic material as a psychiatric approach to emotional problems in children. *American Journal of Orthopsychiatry*, 1937, *1*, 283-300.

Bills, R. E.: Non-directive play therapy with retarded readers. *Journal of Counseling Psychology*, 1950, *2*, 140-149.

Bradley, C., and Bosquet, E. S.: Uses of books for psychotherapy with children. *American Journal of Orthopsychiatry*, 1936, *6*, 23-31.

Cole, N. R.: Exploring psychodrama at fifth grade level. In R. B. Haas (Ed.): *Psychodrama and Sociodrama in American Education*. New York: Beacon House, 1949, pp. 243-245.

Conn, J. H.: The child reveals himself through play. *Mental Hygiene*, 1939, *23*, 49-69.

Davis, R. G.: Group therapy and social acceptance in a first-second grade. *Elementary School Journal*, 1948, *49*, 210-223.

Drabkova, H.: Experiences resulting from clinical use of psychodrama with children. *Group Psychotherapy*, 1966, *19*, 32-36.

Dreikurs, R., and Sonstegard, M.: The Adlerian or teleoanalytic group counseling approach. In G. M. Gazda (Ed.): *Basic Approaches to Group Psychotherapy and Group Counseling*. Springfield, Ill.: Charles C Thomas, 1968. pp. 197-232.

Fleming, L., and Snyder, W. U.: Social and personal changes following nondirective group play therapy. *American Journal of Orthopsychiatry*, 1947, *17*, 101-116.

Gabriel, B.: An experiment in group treatment. *American Journal of Orthopsychiatry*, 1939, *9*, 146-169.

Gazda, G. M.: A functional approach to group counseling. In G. M. Gazda (Ed.): *Basic Approaches to Group Psychotherapy and Group Counseling*. Springfield, Ill.: Charles C Thomas, 1968. pp. 263-303.

Gazda, G. M., and Folds, J. M.: *Group Guidance: A Critical Incidents Approach*. Chicago: Follett, 1968.

Gildea, M. C. L.: School mental health: Orientation methods and screening. In M. Krugman (Ed.): *Orthopsychiatry and the School.* New York: American Orthopsychiatry Association, 1958. pp. 131-134.

Ginott, H.: Play therapy: A theoretical framework. *International Journal of Group Psychotherapy,* 1958, *8,* 410-418.

Gitelson, M.: Clinical experience with play therapy. *American Journal of Orthopsychiatry,* 1938, *8,* 466-478.

Gitelson, M.: Section on "play therapy." *American Journal of Orthopsychiatry,* 1938, *8,* 499-524.

Glanz, E. C., and Hayes, R. W.: *Groups in Guidance.* (2nd ed.) Boston: Allyn & Bacon, 1967.

Goldman, L.: Group guidance: Content and process. *Personnel and Guidance Journal,* 1962, *40,* 518-522.

Haas, R. B.: A summary of findings from an exploratory study, "sociodrama in education." *Sociatry,* 1948, *2,* 232-241.

Haas, R. B.: The consultant in sociometry and sociodrama speaks. In R. B. Haas (Ed.): *Psychodrama and Sociodrama in American Education.* New York: Beacon House, 1949. pp. 257-268.

Hambridge, G., Jr.: Structured play therapy. *American Journal of Orthopsychiatry,* 1955, *25,* 601-617.

Heinicke, C., and Goldman, A.: Research on psychotherapy with children: A review and suggestions for further study. *Journal of Orthopsychiatry,* 1960, *30,* 483-493.

Hewitt, H., and Gildea, M. C. L.: An experiment in group psychotherapy. *American Journal of Orthopsychiatry,* 1945, *15,* 112-127.

Jennings, H. H.: Sociodrama as an educative process. In *Fostering Mental Health in Our Schools.* Washington, D. C.: Association for Supervision and Curriculum Development, N.E.A., 1950. pp. 260-285.

Levy, D. M.: Use of play technique as experimental procedure. *American Journal of Orthopsychiatry,* 1933, *3,* 266-277.

Levy, D. M.: Release therapy in young children. *Psychiatry,* 1938, *1,* 387-390.

Lifton, W. M.: Group centered counseling. In G. M. Gazda (Ed.): *Basic Approaches to Group Psychotherapy and Group Counseling.* Springfield, Ill.: Charles C Thomas, 1968, pp. 233-262.

Mowrer, O. H.: On the dual nature of learning—A reinterpretation of "conditioning" and "problem-solving." *Harvard Educational Review,* 1947, *17,* 102-148.

Murphy, G.: Play as a counselor's tool. *School Counselor,* 1960, *8,* 53-58.

Piaget, J.: *Play, Dreams, and Imitation in Childhood.* New York: W. W. Norton, 1951.

Rubin, E. Z., and Simson, C. B.: A special class program for the emotionally disturbed child in school: A proposal. *American Journal of Orthopsychiatry,* 1960, *30,* 144-153.

Schiffer, M.: A therapeutic play group in a public school. *Mental Hygiene,* 1957, *41,* 185-193.

Schiffer, M.: The therapeutic group in the elementary school. In M. Krugman (Ed.): *Orthopsychiatry and the School.* New York: American Orthopsychiatry Association, 1958. pp. 70-95.

Schiffer, M.: The use of the seminar in training teachers and counselors as leaders of therapeutic play groups for maladjusted children. *American Journal of Orthopsychiatry,* 1960, *30,* 154-165.

Shoals, M.: Psychodrama in the schools. *Psychodrama Monographs,* 1947, No. 10.

Solomon, J. C.: Active play therapy. *American Journal of Orthopsychiatry,* 1938, *8,* 479-497.

Strang, R.: *Group Work in Education.* New York: Harper, 1958.

Woltmann, A.: Concepts of play therapy techniques. *American Journal of Orthopsychiatry,* 1955, *25,* 771-783.

III

ACTIVITY GROUP COUNSELING

JOHN D. BLAKEMAN AND SHERMAN R. DAY

THE FIRST COUNSELING programs were composed primarily of vocational and educational planning with emphasis upon vocational advisement. Patterson (1966) points out that the emphasis was upon a rational, cognitive approach to vocational counseling. In the 1940's, the counseling movement experienced the impact of a strong influence away from the logical, rational approach to an emphasis upon the value of the interpersonal relationship. Counseling moved away from the professional concern for vocational problem solving to concern for the personal-social-emotional problems of the individual. The debate over whether or not the public schools should provide this type of counseling is far from being ended. However, there is evidence that the public schools are now beginning to accept the counselor as a person who does perform personal-social-emotional counseling.

How far should the school go in providing counseling services? Allinsmith and Goethals (1962) claimed that it is the obligation of the school to aid in the development of healthy personalities and the responsibility of the guidance specialist to carry out this responsibility. Landy and Scanlan (1962) have suggested that the school provide "relationship counseling" which they contend is "more supportive and leads to some insight with actual re-educative goals." Patterson (1967) contends that the public schools are the perfect places for social-emotional-personal counseling. He bases this contention on the fact that the child spends a greater proportion of his daily life in the school than in any other institution. Therefore, the child is accessible to the school counselor. Patterson further states that because of the lack of community counseling services and because of the fact that vocational counseling cannot be differentiated from personal counseling, the school is the prime institution in which counseling can take place. Patterson (1962) points out that the counselor should be prepared to work with disturbed children in school, and if there is a need to refer every child who acts disturbed, the counselor should not be working as a counselor.

Recognizing the need for personal-social-emotional counseling in the schools, psychologists and educators have been concerned for quite some time with treatment procedures for the child who does not respond to traditional counseling techniques. Many labels have been used to describe the problem child including juvenile delinquent, classroom deviant, culturally disadvantaged, culturally different, impoverished, acting out, behavioral problem, hyperactive, the withdrawn child, and the like. In spite of the labels that are used, these children seem to exhibit similar characteristics. They include withdrawn behavior, inability to get along with peers, aggressiveness, immaturity, excessive nervousness, short attention span, negative relationship with the school officials, overly concerned with sex, cheating, lying, stealing, not attracted to middle class values or style of life and/or rejection of middle class standards, anti-intellectual, alienated from society, and low self-esteem (Clancy and Smitter, 1965; Riessman, 1962; Rorher, 1964). In addition, a high rate of social maladjustment, behavioral disturbance, and academic retardation are characteristic of the "problem" child in the school (Gordon and Wilkerson, 1966).

School counselors have been charged with the responsibility of working with the "problem" student in the school setting (Mink, 1966). However, counselors who have counseled with these students continually report frustration from their lack of success. The authors believe that one reason for the counselor's lack of success with this population in the school setting is that he is seen as an adult authority much like the principal, truant officer, or probation officer. A typical counseling office arrangement (i.e., chair-desk-chair) and the interview technique predominantly used by school counselors only serves to reinforce the authoritarian position of the school counselor. Counselors report that many of their interviews with "problem" students consist entirely of "yes sir" or "no sir" responses by the counselee. Further, the cultural differences between the counselor and the counselee have served as an additional communication barrier and inhibited the effective counseling relationship (Kvaraceus, 1967). It seems, therefore, that new communication models need to be developed for counseling with the "problem" child.

Calia (1966) spoke about the problem of counseling the disadvantaged child. He contends:

> The counseling process as currently conceived is highly incongruous with the life style of the poor. The counseling interview is deemed to be singularly inappropriate. The introspective and verbal demands of the dyadic encounter, and the phenomenon of assumed similarity and the necessity for self-referral, all serve to vitiate the counselor's effectiveness (p. 100).[1]

Gordon (1964) summarizes the concern of the professional counselor for this population by stating:

> As an educational psychologist and a specialist in guidance, I have the feeling that I should say something practical about counseling disadvantaged children. However, I must say that I am not at all certain that we know how best to counsel or that counseling is our most effective tool of guided behavior development and change (p. 281).[2]

One cannot ignore the need for professional help by this population. It is reported that in some schools, a majority of the teacher's time is related to keeping discipline (Deutsch, 1960; Olsen, 1965). Bonney (1960) contends that the number one concern of the classroom teacher is the hyperactive, hostile, aggressive student who acts out his emotions in the classroom. It is a small wonder that many of these students find their way into the counselor's office for personal-social counseling.

Very few research studies report favorable research results with the "difficult" adolescent. Indeed, the low possibilities of

---

[1] From Calia, V. P.: The culturally deprived client: A reformation of the counselor's role. *Journal of Counseling Psychology*, 1966, *13*, 100-106. Courtesy of American Psychological Assoc., Inc., Washington, D. C.

[2] From Gordon, E. W.: Counseling socially disadvantaged children. In F. Riessman, J. Cohen, and A. Pearl (Eds.): *Mental Health of the Poor*. 1966. Courtesy of The Free Press of Glencoe, New York, New York.

success with this population may account for the paucity of work in this area. Nevertheless, one cannot ignore the fact that every school contains a certain percentage of these adolescents who desperately need counseling and guidance. Some evidence is available that new counseling techniques and counselor training procedures can be developed which are effective with the "problem" child (Krumboltz and Thoreson, 1964; Slack, 1960).

A summary of the literature reveals two important suggestions for school counselors in their efforts to assist the "problem" child in school. First, it seems clear that good *communication* patterns are essential for effective counseling; however, continued reliance upon the verbal skills of the counselee tends to retard effective communication (Calia, 1966; Kvaraceus, 1967; Riessman, 1962). Tyler (1964) suggests that we move away from the traditional counseling approaches which focus upon the interview. She contends that talk in a natural setting is more akin to life style of the individual in counseling and should be used to more advantage by the counselor. Some authors have maintained that the "problem" child is nonverbal; however, Riessman (1962) found these students to be quite spontaneous and relaxed when placed in a familiar, natural setting. He reports that, although the quality of the language was lacking, students were far from nonverbal when not confined to the traditional counseling setting.

The second suggestion for school counselors gleaned from the professional literature points to the use of *group techniques* for effective counseling of the "problem" child. One cannot study the literature on boys' gangs without coming to the conclusion that these youngsters are ingenious and resourceful. At the same time, the literature indicates that these students are capable of meaningful, loyal, interpersonal relationships within a group setting. The counselor would do well to capitalize on the identification processes involved in these relationships through the use of a group approach to counseling. Psychologists have maintained that the peer group influences are very strong during the adolescent development stage. Therefore, any decision to modify behavior which originates within a counseling group is more likely to yield positive results than decisions which are made for the counselees by those in authoritarian roles. The group becomes its own enforcing agency and stresses conformity to its new norms (Bonney, 1965). Ohlsen (1964) summarizes his experience in counseling adolescents by stating:

> Group counseling seems particularly appropriate for adolescents whose special needs include conformity with and acceptance by their peer group, opportunity to share ideas, and to obtain reaction from the peers, occasion to participate in worthwhile activities, help to define meaningful life roles and independence from adults, especially from parents. These needs can best be satisfied within the effective counseling group (p. 148).[3]

The use of activity group counseling is, in effect, a concession to the method of learning which many problem children have characteristically employed. The counselor responds to the client's immediate behavior in a direct and objective manner devoid of criticism or reprimand. This presents the adult counselor in a different light. Hence the adolescent's usual defiant responses are inappropriate for the new counseling situation. The counselor provides a model for which a new and different set of responses may be developed. In order for the adolescent to resolve the dissonance between his previous beliefs and the actions of the counselor, he must either change his behavior appropriately or deny the validity of the counselor's unconditional positive regard and acceptance of him. Since change is more psychologically economical, the student will alter his patterns of behavior and conceptualizations of adult authority. When this change occurs, a counseling relationship will develop.

It is safe to assume that the counselee will continually test the counselor for acceptance and sincerity. The counselor will encounter an attitude and response set that the counselee has maintained for most of his life and for which there has been frequent reinforcement. It will indeed be a challenge to the counselor to accept this testing by the student and yet maintain his objectivity of response patterns in the counseling setting.

Gazda (1965) listed five unique positive features of group counseling which make it an attractive treatment for many clients, including adolescents:

---

[3] From Ohlsen, M. M.: *Guidance Services in the Modern School.* 1964. Courtesy of Harcourt, Brace & World, New York, New York.

1. A group provides the individual the opportunity to give as well as to receive help.
2. A group member has the opportunity to learn new ways of attacking his problems by observing others in the group deal with similar problems.
3. A group serves as a testing ground for ideas and behavior before applying them to "outside-the-group living."
4. A group provides the participant the opportunity to interact with several different individuals and to obtain feedback as to how he affects them.
5. Group support can be very strong and thus provide the impetus that an individual may need to resolve a given problem. (p. 16)[4]

ACTIVITY GROUP COUNSELING DEFINED

The authors have abstracted two constructs from the literature i.e., the need for communication through a natural, spontaneous activity different from a typical counseling setting and the use of group counseling techniques from which to base a counseling methodology for school counselors. We have called this process *activity group counseling*. We define it as follows:

Activity group counseling refers to the group process which improves communication through natural, spontaneous activity whereby peers participate in the developmental, behavioral, and attitudinal concerns of the individual members of the counseling group.

Activity counseling is an outgrowth of play techniques developed by Axline (1947), Slavson (1954), Moustakas (1955), and Ginott (1961). Just as children prefer playing with dolls, puppets, clay, and finger paints, the adolescent prefers certain activities more appropriate to his age level. Activities such as basketball, football, swimming, or darts appeal to most adolescent boys. They present a realistic enjoyable situation for the release of emotional feelings. Activities such as crafts, painting, wood shop, or home economics are also akin to the likes of adolescents.

The activity serves as the medium for spontaneous expression of behavior. The students act out their feelings and emotions during the activity. It is assumed that typical, self-defeating

[4] From Gazda, G. M.: New trends in counseling. *School Counselor,* 1965, *13*, 14-18. Courtesy of American School Counselors Assoc., a division of the American Personnel and Guidance Association, Washington, D. C.

behavior patterns of the "problem" child will manifest themselves in a spontaneous, natural setting. The emphasis in the activity is the relationship rather than the talk required in traditional counseling. For example, aggressive children tend to be aggressive in the activities, while withdrawn children will typically retreat. The counselor helps the student become aware of the effects of his behavior by reflecting the behavioral dynamics to the group. The group assists in this task by discussing the effects of this individual. The peer reaction becomes an important quality in activity group counseling. The group is encouraged to participate in group discussions and focus on personal-social-emotional behavior, thus the counseling group is different from other clubs and organizations in school. The focus upon feelings, emotions, and peer reactions to behavior becomes the norm of the group in counseling.

We do not intend to imply that the concept of counseling in groups in an activity setting is original. Professionals from other mental health disciplines have utilized this approach with reported success in many settings. For example, adaptions of play therapy techniques have been used successfully in fresh air camps, child guidance clinics, and other institutions. The intent of this chapter, however, is to develop the rationale and methods for the implementation of activity techniques into the regular school counseling program—which is new.

PIONEER EFFORTS

Joseph Galkin (1937) was concerned with supplementary techniques to the child guidance clinic with which he was associated. Galkin contended that case work was a very sterile way of dealing with children. He proposed that more real situations that are more akin to the natural patterns of the child be established. He established a camp in New York to deal with boys between the ages of eight and sixteen. The typical treatment length was three to nine months. Treatment focused on the behavior and personality problems, and stress was placed upon maintaining and developing a therapeutic environment consisting of informal relationships.

The personnel involved in the camp had the opportunity to appraise the boy's behavior in case conferences with psychiatrists and other mental health workers. Galkin, himself, contributed the therapeutic value of natural, spontaneous relationships which were not distasteful to the clients. Galkin concluded that the activity group experience provided significant positive results in most behavioral areas.

Betty Gabriel (1939) also examined the potential of activity group work with young children. She established a group relationship with clients previously scheduled for individual work. Field trips, clay work, painting, and similar activities were provided for the group. Limits of behavior were established to reduce the danger to individuals and property; however, a permissive, accepting atmosphere was maintained. Topics of a personal nature were discussed openly by the group with the activity media leading the group members into deeper free discussion. As group cohesiveness developed, the therapist began to interpret behavior to the youngsters. While individual treatments supplemented the group approach, Gabriel felt that activity treatment provided the emphasis for behavior change.

One of the earliest references to activity group therapy was made by Moreno in 1946 in his discussion of sociodrama and psychodrama. Moreno's treatment placed emphasis on contrived situational events and controlling the behavior of participants through association with these events. Moreno contended that placing children in real situations would necessarily lead to both good and bad behavior. Therefore, his method eliminated the bad behavior-producing situation and focused on the social behavior that was valuable to the individual (Moreno, 1946).

S. R. Slavson (1954) pioneered the activity group therapy approach and described the process in his book, *Re-educating the Delinquent*. Slavson's book deals with his experiences in 1935 while working in a school for delinquent girls. The girls were between the ages of eleven and eighteen and had been diagnosed as institutionalized delinquents. Slavson saw that individual work would not be accepted by the girls and decided that group techniques were most appropriate for this situation. He allowed the subjects more unsupervised freedom and utilized cohesiveness of the group to effect security. The group discussions centered on the negative behaviors exhibited by the girls in the school setting.

Slavson's work was evaluated as positive by both staff and administration and resulted in changes in philosophy and policy of the school. Behavioral improvements were noted by both therapists and the staff.

Stranahan, Schwartzman, and Atkin (1957) report the treating of emotionally disturbed delinquent boys and girls in a clinical setting. Care was given to group selection; in addition, clinical diagnosis was established for those in therapy. Individual treatment was ruled out because of the suspiciousness, anxiety, and poor verbalization which characterized this group of youngsters. Some of the boys lacked identification with male models. These boys initially rejected the male counselors; however, effective identification was established by living out experiences with adult therapists. Stages of development were noted by the authors in discussing how limits were set. Interpretation of feeling was the major therapeutic technique. Significant symptom reduction was reported in both home and school.

Coolidge and Grunebaum (1964) reviewed a case in which an eighteen-year-old, nonverbal girl was successfully treated in activity group therapy. They found that adolescents often have problems, the causes of which are not easy to identify. In essence, these problems are preverbal, thus group activities provide a vehicle for communication and effective treatment.

Davids (1955) described a ten-year-old, emotionally disturbed Negro boy who was helped by activity group therapy. In addition to the treatment of the child, case work services were provided for the boy's family. The boy's tantrums, compulsions, fears, and anxieties were alleviated through activity group therapy; his self-image became more positive; and his behavior at home and at school improved.

Lieberman (1964) found that activity groups can develop into interview groups. While working with adolescent girls, she observed that the group became more and more interested in sex themes, i.e., menstruation, petting, and so forth. These girls verbalized their concerns when they began to feel that they were being helped as their expressions were interpreted.

Use of the activity group approach as a means of treating hospitalized youths also has been investigated. Westman (1963) reported positive results achieved by involving institutionalized adolescents (mental patients) in a Boy Scout experience. The opportunities for the boys to experience treatment as persons of worth and belonging in a reality situation had significant meaning to participants and resulted in improved human functioning.

Rybach (1963) utilized a technique similar to Westman's in working with teen-age patients who were hospitalized. Rybach induced them to participate in forming rules and regulations for their own control. The therapeutic design of this activity was not disclosed to the participants; however, much improvement in attitude and behavior was subsequently involved in the activity.

Beard, Goertzel, and Pearce (1958) reported that psychiatrists had considerable success in working with adult mental patients using the activity approach in treatment. Male patients ranging in age from sixteen to twenty-four had been placed in the custodial care of a mental hospital. These patients had been diagnosed as schizophrenic and had not responded to any traditional therapeutic treatments. Therapists began by developing positive relationships on an individual basis and then moved into group activities. The treatment was quite diverse, ranging from working mathematics problems to playing soccer. The patients all showed improvement in behavior following activity group counseling.

Studies by Ramsey (1964) and Shannon and Snortum (1961) illustrate the success of the activity approach. Ramsey recommended camping as part of the treatment for hospitalized patients. Seventy-five per cent of 685 patients involved in the camp experiences were rated by their physicians as making improvement ranging from minimal to complete functioning. According to Ramsey, the camp experience was responsible for the discharge of eighteen patients. Shannon and Snortum also found activities to be effective in treating institutionalized patients. They reported the patients' use of activities to gain acceptance from their peers and to develop group cohesiveness which, in turn, produced a feeling of being needed.

Several studies reported favorable results in the use of the activity group approach to treat personal-social concerns of adolescents. Gump and Sutton-Smith (1955) hypothesized that the activity itself contained a reality factor capable of producing behavior change. This hypothesis was formulated from observations of adolescents in camp settings. Gump and Sutton-Smith proposed that behavior in swimming varied from that in crafts and concluded that an activity could be selected specifically as a therapeutic tool for influencing a child's behavior.

Fleischl (1962) observed that self-esteem can be improved through creative activity. He reported that increased awareness of other group members grew out of situations which closely resembled life.

Levy (1950) attempted an out-of-door therapeutic treatment for adolescent boys. His study grew out of the inability to establish healthy relationships in traditional therapy. Levy enlisted the help of two nonprofessional friends who were found to be, in his words, "natural therapists." Levy followed a treatment philosophy suggested by Sullivan in his writing in interpersonal relationships. We have summarized the results of Levy's study as follow:

1. The out-of-doors provides an environment where children can have unlimited opportunity for free, spontaneous activity.
2. The setting was unusually comfortable for the therapists to work in because of their personal interest in out-of-door activity. A large number of possibilities exist in the activities such as these for children. Concrete incidents of positive behavior can be rewarded in this setting.

ACTIVITY GROUP COUNSELING RESEARCH IN THE SCHOOL

Research dealing with activity group counseling with adolescents, preadolescents, and adults in institutionalized settings and child guidance clinics is plentiful; however, one finds a scarcity of research on the application of the activity group approach to the school setting.

Koenig (1949) described activity group therapy employed with children who needed assistance in social skills in the classroom. She limited her group to ten students who met one hour per week for six months. Children who exhibited delinquent, aggressive, or withdrawn behavior were selected for the groups. Classroom teachers from elementary schools referred the youngsters on the basis of behavior difficulties. Numerous activities such as board games and recreational play were utilized in the treatment, and a wide range of objects were available for the children to manipulate. Koenig reported only one child who failed to make behavioral improvement. She stated that the most important contributor to the activity success was "the emotional security derived from living in a stable, well regulated environment where one is accepted and has some worthwhile work to accomplish" (pp. 268-269).

Alexander (1964) reported a case study of a child who had been involved in activity group therapy in his school. He found that the key to improvement of the individual was the relationship that developed between the child and the therapist. These two studies represent the limited application of the activity group principle to school-age children prior to the research by the authors which is described below.

Day (1967) studied the use of activity group counseling on culturally disadvantaged, behavioral problem boys referred for counseling by classroom teachers. The subjects were twenty-five culturally disadvantaged Negro boys, ranging in age from eleven to fourteen. They were initially selected through the use of behavior ratings by classroom teachers. Each teacher in the school, by means of ratings, selected the boys in their classes whom they considered to be behavioral problems. The students that were referred by two or more teachers were further screened by the use of the Hollingshed Index of Social Position. This instrument was used to ascertain the student's social position—culturally disadvantaged. The sample was divided into two groups designated experimental and control. The experimental group consisted of thirteen boys while the control group consisted of twelve boys. Both of these groups were further divided into counseling groups of five or six.

The experimental group met in activity counseling three times a week for five weeks. During this time, the control group received no counseling or guidance activities. Immediately after termination of the experimental groups, activity group counseling was provided for the control group. These students served as their own control for the purpose of statistical evaluation. Data were collected from both experimental and control group subjects at the beginning of the study, at the end of the first phase of the experiment, and at the end of the total study.

A criterion instrument used in measuring the change of classroom behavior was the Haggerty-Olson-Wickman Behavior Rating Schedule B (HOW). The criterion instrument used in measuring change in peer acceptance was a sociometric instrument designed by the investigator. The null hypothesis was posed in each case. Differences in mean gains for classroom social behavior, classroom emotional behavior, and total classroom behavior were calculated for the experimental versus the control group and for the control group during the control phase versus the control group during the counseling phase.

The results indicate that those students receiving activity group counseling showed favorable gains in classroom social behavior and total classroom behavior (p. 05). Differences in mean gains for classroom emotional behavior were not significant in either phase of experimental investigation. Differences in mean gains of positive and negative choices by peers were also found as a result of activity group counseling, but the differences were not significant. Day concluded:

1. Activity group counseling has an effect on classroom behavior of culturally disadvantaged, behavioral problem students. Social behaviors were particularly affected by experience of activity group counseling. Emotional behavior was also affected by activity group counseling, although non-significantly.
2. Written evaluation by teachers confirmed that twenty-three of the twenty-five subjects were seen as significantly improved in classroom behavior.
3. Activity group counseling was seen by the participants as a very positive experience. All of the subjects in this study expressed a desire to continue counseling in groups. Each student rated the experience as being both helpful and pleasant.

4. Activity group counseling can be conducted within the confines of the typical setting using facilities in the school (1967, p. 103).

Blakeman (1967) investigated the effects of activity group counseling on the classroom behavior of seventh-and eighth-grade problem boys of Caucasian origin who ranged in age from eleven to fourteen. Forty-nine boys were recommended by teachers and then interviewed as possible participants for the study. From this group forty boys volunteered to participate. This investigation included group activity meetings which were held weekly after school for one hour over a period of six weeks. The activities included touch football, golf, table tennis, swimming, and visits to a nearby confectionery. Criterion instrument for behavioral improvement were the Self Evaluation Picture Tests (SEPT) and the Haggerty-Olson-Wickman Behavioral Rating Schedule (HOW). An independent examination of the experimental group indicated that activity group treatment had a positive effect upon the self-evaluation and classroom behavior of these behavioral problem boys. Evaluation of the data further indicated that experimental subjects changed in the desired direction, and no regression was noted over a four and one-half month period. Blakeman concluded:

1. It can be stated with reasonable sureness that activity group treatment effects desirable changes in boys' self-evaluation to significant degrees.
2. Graduate training programs can easily incorporate activity group counseling experiences and practicum courses for trainees. A variety of activities seem appropriate as a setting for activity group treatment. All of these are available within the school confines (pp. 69-70).

SUMMARY OF RESEARCH

If the opinions of professional therapists are to give us direction and encouragement, we have substantial support from research and theory to believe that activity group counseling is a useful tool for behavior modification of adolescents. Behavioral problems which manifest themselves in varied forms of suspicion, lack of trust, inadequate verbalization, and ineffective social skills appear more amenable to activity group counseling, especially for the preadolescent, than do traditional methods of counseling. Activity group counseling provides for group interaction in a reality situation devoid of threat or anxiety. The approach to counseling preadolescents and adolescents through activity groups may be employed by group counselors who, themselves, feel comfortable in an action-oriented environment. Psychologically skilled personnel should be involved in selection of the group participants. Furthermore, since certain manifest behavior patterns warrant different treatment methods, such as individual counseling, therapy, psychological assistance combined with medical help, consultation seems desirable.

A final conclusion based on the experiences of the authors suggests the possibility of the school environment as being one of the best possible areas for providing a natural means of assisting the preadolescent and adolescent student with an adjustment problem. The available activity areas, such as playgrounds, gymnasiums, art rooms, shops, discussion rooms, home economics laboratories, libraries, lunch rooms, stages, and science laboratories, seem to substantiate further the potential application of activity group counseling in the school.

RATIONALE FOR BEHAVIOR CHANGE

Several philosophical systems are available for describing characteristics and interactions of group treatment. Each approach claims some expertness in the changing and modification of behavior. One such explanation of change relates the counselor as a behavioral model for group members. Members observe the leader, thus different ways of behaving becomes apparent. Another explanation is that members are "conditioned" to act differently as a result of the group experience and the interaction with leader and peers. Reality testing and roleplaying are also offered as prime reasons for behavioral change in activity group counseling. The authors acknowledge that all of these phenomena are important to and often occur in a group counseling experience. However, they believe that the fundamental contributor to behavioral change is the significant relationships that develop within the group.

In some groups, the major contributor to change will be the relationships among group members; but in most cases where adolescents are involved in groups, the major relationship contributing to change will be between counselor and individual group member. The activity to be used serves as a vehicle through which relationships develop. Much latitude for involvement is afforded the counselor and the group members in the activity setting. *Involvement* is the key ingredient in significant positive relationships. Thus, many activities would quite naturally and easily provide numerous opportunities for the counselor to become therapeutically involved with the group members. The only limit to therapeutic involvement through activities, it seems would be the counselor's and group members' ingenuity and perhaps available physical facilities.

Many adolescents and preadolescents are visibly threatened and suspicious in the presence of adult authority figures. This is most obvious in the instances of forced referrals to counseling. Placing young people in counseling situations marked by rigidity and formal structure adds further to their distrust of authority figures. The activity approach does not emphasize "treatment" as such and is observed therefore to be less threatening to those in preadolescent and early adolescent age groups. Movement from a lack of trust in adults to trust in them through an activity experience is viewed as growth and evidence of change in a positive direction.

Support for the importance of the relationship in counseling comes from several sources. Gibb and Gibb (1968) stated that "therapy takes place in a growth relationship. Therapy is a relationship, a social process. All relationships which are growth-producing and defense-reductive are therapeutic. . ." (pp. 97-98). Fiedler (1950), several years ago, was aware of the contribution of the *relationship* to growth in persons seeking help. He conducted investigations to determine the characteristics of the relationship created by therapists from different theoretical schools. Glasser (1965) advocates the treatment of patients using a reality therapy approach which also seems to be largely *relationship* oriented. Rogers (1951, 1959) has probably been responsible, more than any other person, for generating research into the importance of the relationship in the helping process. In his earliest writing, (Rogers, 1942) recognized the possibility of activities and play. He suggested:

> One area which needs to be explored is the adaptation of play therapy techniques to adolescents and adults. Such techniques offer an easy and symbolic way of expressing feeling and conflict, and if they can be adapted to the older individuals, they should be helpful devices. To the extent to which these techniques leave the client entirely free to express his attitudes and provide easy and comfortable ways of doing so, they are helpful (p. 95).[5]

Rogers (1957) lists the following six specific conditions which he feels are necessary to promote change within a client.

1. Two people meet in a psychological encounter.
2. The first person, the client, is in a state of incongruence, vulnerable, and anxious.
3. The second person, the counselor, is integrated in the relationship.
4. The counselor experiences unconditional positive regard for the client.
5. The counselor experiences empathic understanding of the client's internal frame of reference and endeavors to communicate this experience to the client.
6. The communication to the client of the counselor's empathic understanding and unconditional positive regard is to a minimal degree achieved (pp. 95-103).[6]

Patterson (1959) views techniques in counseling as being secondary to the relationship. He sees counseling and psychotherapy akin to other human relationships and believes that often counseling is described in ways that make it seem unnecessarily complicated and esoteric. Patterson entertains the possibility that counselors give themselves to the relationship. The counselor gives time, interest, and attitudes which, although they may be considered intangible, are nevertheless essential to the counseling relationship. Patterson states, however, that the counseling relationship is more intense and concentrated than a social

---

[5] From Rogers, C. R.: *Counseling and Psychotherapy.* 1942. Courtesy of Houghton Mifflin, Boston, Massachusetts.

[6] From Rogers, C. R.: The necessary and sufficient conditions of therapeutic personality change. *Journal of Consulting Psychology,* 1957, *21,* 95-103. Courtesy of American Psychological Assoc., Inc., Washington, D. C.

relationship and, to an extent, is planned so that special assistance is provided by a healthy person to one who is not meeting his basic needs and goals. The removal of threat, according to Patterson, is essentially responsible for the client being able to look more deeply into himself and expose himself to the counselor. In order to provide a therapeutic relationship, Patterson feels that the counselor needs a sufficiently positive self-concept.

Jourard (1964) believes that counseling is more than symptom removal. He views it as helping persons find their being and identity. He implied the importance of the counseling relationship in meeting this goal when he described the relationship with the counselor as, "one which invites challenges, or permits the emergence of authentic being in him." He describes the importance of client trust in the relationship and views effective counselors as responding honestly to clients in a spirit of good will and within certain limits of safety.

More recently Carkhuff and Berenson (1967) cited several research studies which reveal that not only are Rogers' conditions important, but the degree to which they are present in a relationship determines whether or not the relationship is facilitative.

In summary, it is our contention that the relationship is the main factor in promoting change. Involvement with persons in mutually satisfying activities enhances the development of this relationship. If one wishes to introduce a particular technique or approach to add to the growth potential of individuals in groups, we feel certain that this intervention will succeed if it contributes to the development of a therapeutic relationship.

GROUND RULES IN ACTIVITY GROUP COUNSELING

Several counselors have devised elaborate ground rules for group experiences (Gendlin, 1968; Ginott, 1961). The authors, themselves, have found that an inordinate amount of time used defining limits serves to reinforce the "authoritarian" system and negates the very essence of relationships with adolescents. We prefer to spend time dealing with positive constructs such as the number of alternatives available to the adolescent. This is not to say that limits will not be tested. However, our limits are fairly well defined by the school setting itself, i.e., no physical violence or abuse to property.

We realize that at times a counselor must have qualities both of "mother" and "father." Sometimes therapeutic tenderness and love are essential for growth. At other times, his experience dictates that limits must be imposed for the good of the group. One example of imposing limits might be in regard to physical punishment occurring to a particular adolescent in a group. The counselor must judge when this abuse is detracting from the helping process and take steps to correct this defect.

THE COUNSELOR'S ROLE IN ACTIVITY GROUP COUNSELING

Since an emphasis in the activity group counseling approach is placed upon the relationships developed within the group, the counselor's major task is to become involved enough to allow relationships to develop. Significant involvement can be described as Rogers (1957) does in his first condition for personality change: Psychological encounter. Gendlin (1968) called this psychological "contact." He explained this as something mutually felt that tells each person in the relationship that he makes a difference to the others in the relationship. The concern, interest, acceptance, and other attitudes which are the core of the relationship are accelerated through direct involvement.

Often the involvement may be accomplished through direct participation as a team member or partner. Some attention should be given to relate to all group members as equally as is possible. Direct competition with group members should be avoided, particularly in early sessions. Competitive confrontations tend to depreciate adolescents' feelings of worthwhileness. In later sessions, when it is clear that the counselor's behavior is spontaneous and that his overall goal is to be helpful, less concern need be given to the effects of leader-member competition. More indirect and subtle means of involvement may be desirable at first or when the leader feels somewhat uncomfortable himself in direct involvement in an activity. Kibitzing and refereeing are examples of ways to becoming involved without the threat of direct confrontation or competition.

The counselor encourages free expression throughout the sessions. The goal is to assist each member to be as openly himself as possible. The counselor can quickly facilitate the openness by demonstrating *his* willingness to be this way. When a group member's actions affect another member's actions, the counselor can either direct the group to a discussion about the incident at that time or make a note to bring it up at a discussion to be held at the end of the activity. Group members are encouraged to give their reactions to the event to help those involved understand how their behavior is perceived by other group members. The counselor must be sensitive to incidents which occur and trust his judgment concerning the most appropriate time to deal with the behavior.

During the activity, the counselor might reflect feelings, argue, cajole, help, clarify feelings, interpret behavior, enlist others' help, and the like. The goal should be a meaningful relationship established through the mutual involvement in the activity. The impact of the relationship will be felt when the counselor's intention to help is communicated to the group members.

The existence of a significant, positive relationship allows the counselor more freedom to confront the group members. In instances where a meaningful relationship does not exist, more defensive behavior by the group members is encountered.

COUNSELEE BEHAVIOR IN ACTIVITY GROUP COUNSELING

Adolescents and preadolescents in traditional group counseling will spend some time becoming acclimated before they can legitimately be called a group. Foley and Bonney (1966) characterize this as a stage of development in the group process called the *establishment stage*. It is during this stage that the group gets to know each other through their verbal and nonverbal behavior. One to four meetings seem necessary for roles and relationships to be worked out.

Earlier experiences with adolescents and preadolescents in counseling groups demonstrated that the first stage of development is a critical one. Youngsters who normally make up counseling groups are those who have problems. They do not identify strongly with adult models and are therefore resistive and defensive. In this stage, limits are tested and counselor sincerity is questioned. Activities which are introduced seem to reduce, considerably, the threat that exists about the experience. The group participants can quickly experience the feeling of acceptance and being special without having to be involved in verbal competition with other group members.

The involvement in the activity with other group members and the leader takes place immediately. The natural reinforcement of behavior which communicates the important feelings the leader has for each group member can begin during the first meeting since activity involvement almost always insures some participation on the part of each group member. Furthermore, the planning of the first activity and following activities demands participation by each member. Even if it is in the passive form of noting or acknowledging consent, each member assists in determining what will happen during each meeting.

Client behavior in activity group counseling is the same spontaneous behavior you would expect to observe in persons participating in game or recreational type activities. The infrequent interventions by the leader and summary discussions at the conclusion of each activity would be the only marked difference that would demonstrate to an observer that the group was special in any way.

SELECTION AND SIZE OF ACTIVITY GROUPS

Group members should always have the opportunity to volunteer for participation and be free to drop out at any time. No coercion of any kind should be used. Each prospective group member should be interviewed individually and informed about the reasons he was selected for possible inclusion in the group. It is helpful to invite persons to participate who have similar manifest symptoms. Behavior problems, test phobias, and chronic tardiness, for example, demonstrate that school groups often have a *common* problem of school failure. If research data are to be collected, each individual should be informed. As nearly as possible, each member should be told the purpose of the research. The parents of each group member should be notified if research data are collected and how it will be used. Although differences will exist in regard to the extent one should go to inform parents, the authors found that maintaining a cooperative relationship with parents is quite feasible. In general, the authors have found that honesty and straight forward communication as to goals and expectations of the group best serve our therapeutic aims.

We have not reached a firm commitment as to the optimum size of activity counseling groups; however, group counselors usually suggest between six and ten members for traditional counseling groups. Groups of this size seem most efficient; nevertheless, success has been achieved with as few as three or four group members. Upper limits of group size have not been tested for activity group counseling and therefore evidence is inconclusive as to ideal size. The authors suggest that the counselor's comfort and ease with specific activities will help him to determine a number compatible with the particular activity.

PROTOCOL OF AN ACTIVITY COUNSELING GROUP

Sixth session—six Negro boys present a crisis situation. The boys are milling around the group room; some reading, others drawing, one throwing darts. J. is very active.

J.—I'm not gonna tell anything in the meeting today because every time I do, R tells————.

R.—I did not tell!

Co.—Let's hear about this.

J.—I am not going to say anything.

R.—He went and shot off his big mouth, and because I told ————now he is mad at me.

J.—Ah Peanut, that isn't either what happened. That isn't the first time you've done this, Peanut. I've been playing with you all day and you've been doing it all along. Every time you touch him he gets mad. Just touch him a little bit and he gets mad; he's a baby.

Co.—What about that, group? How would you handle this?

W.—J. is to blame; he is always to blame. He's a great big bully.

J.—I didn't touch him. I know what I'm gonna do about it; I'm just not gonna associate with anybody in this group anymore.

R.—Don't worry; it will pass over.

J.—No, it won't pass over, R. I'm the only one around this school that even likes you a little bit and I don't like you now. You're gonna be so lonely. I'm the best friend you got and you did me dirty and that's all I'm gonna have to do with you.

Co.—It sounds like J. is pretty mad this time.

M.—I think they are both at fault. I think they are both babies.

Co.—Let's talk about the basketball game we played yesterday.

J.—I'm not gonna talk. Every time I talk, somebody tells on me. I've been in the office more than anybody this year, more than any of you punks.

Co.—J., it sounds like maybe you are blaming R. for some of your problems.

J.—This is part of the office and every time I may do something wrong, R. goes to————and tells him all about it.

Co.—Do you consider this part of the office? Is this like the principal's office?

J.—It was before you came. I don't mind if he tells you, but I don't want him telling————, and I don't want him telling————.

R.—J., you think I am the cause of all your problems.

J.—The way I feel about it, if I weren't around you everything would be all right. That's what I'm gonna do; stay away from you.

Co.—J., it sounds like R. is responsible for everything you have had to go wrong this year.

J.—Most all of 'em, anyway.

Co.—Most all of them?

J.—Yes, all of them. Everything I've been in trouble with is 'cause of him.

Co.—It sounds like J. and R. have had everything to say so far. What do some of the rest of you think? I wonder if some of the other boys might not be able to help you out.

J.—Every time I see two or three boys beat up on him, fight him, jump on him, I help him. Now, first time things go wrong, he runs in and tells————. I'm through with him.

Co.—We don't seem to be getting very far with this argument; why don't we try something. Why don't we try J. and R. just being quiet for a minute and let some of the other boys give some of their opinions of how they might handle a situation like this.

J.—No, I'm not through yet. I want to talk some more. I don't like Peanut, and I'm not having any more to do with him.

R.—I think Mr. Co. has a good idea; let's try that.

T.—I think they both got problems. I think they both need to work on 'em.

M.—I think we ought to put them together and let them fight it out.

Co.—It seems to be a lot of buzzing, but no one wants to say anything directly to J. or R. about this situation. I get the idea that all of you would like to but you're kinda frightened of what they might say back.

J.—I think the way to settle this whole thing is if I don't associate with R. anymore. When he gets tired of not associating with me, he'll come around and say, "Let's make friends again; then we'll be friends."

Co.—I'm still puzzled about your saying R. is responsible for all your problems.

J.—Yes, he is. And even though you want me to say something, I'm not gonna say nothing different. He is responsible for all my problems. Let's do something different; I'm tired of this. I don't want to be talking all day long. I'm mad at this group.

Co.—It seems like J. doesn't feel like the group is satisfying him any more. How do the rest of you feel?

Group—It's great; it's what we want. Let's do it.

W.—Let's get J. out of the group if he doesn't like it.

H.—If he wants out, let's get him out.

L.—Yea, let's get him out, if he doesn't want to be in the group; let's get him out.

Co.—I guess the boys are saying, J., that the door is open.

J.—Well, one thing about this group is that when we do play basketball or football, we got a sorry bunch of players. None of them really want to play ball. They're just a bunch of goof-offs. We got a sorry bunch of players.

M.—That's what you say. You shoot all the time anyway, how would you know? You never pass it to anyone.

M.—Why don't you try to teach some of the boys how to play, rather than chewing at them all the time?

R.—Well, I'd like to say something. I tell you this. When J. has the ball, even if you're wide open, he won't pass it to you. He won't pass it to any little boys. All he wants to do is shoot or pass it to one of the big boys. He keeps on dribbling like he don't even hear. All he does is shoot.

M.—I think J. and I are the best basketball players in here, and I think we play harder than any of the other boys. I think J. doesn't like the other boys. He never passes. I try at least to be good to them.

J.—Yeah, W., L., and T., they're no good. They won't even play. They lose interest in the game, and if you don't keep on them all the time, they won't even play. No sense to pass to them, anyway. They just dribble and lose it. They're no good, anyway.

L.—The group wasn't formed just for basketball. There is other reasons, too. Someone else might be good in football. You just want to be the hog in everything you do, J.

Co.—It seems like some of you boys felt like being good in basketball was the main purpose in the group, while others seem to think that there are other purposes in the group.

T.—Yeah, keep us out of trouble.

J.—I'd like to talk now. Now, you say I don't pass the ball, but who in here does pass the ball. Every time I pass the ball to T. or W., they lose the ball. Every time. So why pass to them? Just lose it if I pass it to them.

W.—What you talking about, boy? You don't even know what you are talking about.

J.—Now you answer that, W. Why should I pass it to you?

J.—Now————if you see somebody that ain't gonna do no good with something that is given to them, why give it to them? Why do it? Why give it to them?

Co.—It seems like J. sees a different purpose for the group. He wants to be a good basketball player and have a basketball team. Some of the rest of you don't feel that way.

M.—Well, I think anybody that don't know how to play ought to learn, and I think that this is a good place to learn to do things. I think J. is wrong. I think we ought to be teaching boys to learn.

J.—The time to learn is not while you're playing the game. The time to learn is on your own in your own yard. Besides that, you can't teach boys that don't want to learn. Some of these boys would rather play dodge, so go let them play dodge, but when they come on a basketball floor, they ought to play basketball and they ought to try to be good. If they don't show a lot of interest, they shouldn't ought to be out there.

W.—I'm no good at basketball, but I think that I'd have a lot of fun playing basketball if J. weren't there.

R.—J. always shoots the ball so when we get back to this meeting, he can just talk all the time and brag about what he did during the game.

Co.—Let's take a look now boys at what we are doing. It seems as though everybody is ganging up against J. and it seems like we're trying to tell him that he's not a very good sport when it comes to playing basketball. I think maybe we're being a little hard on him.

J.—Don't worry about me. I don't feel bad.

M.—I think this is good because I think J. needs help. I think he needs help badly not only in basketball but all over.

J.—I don't think I need no help.

M.—Yes, you do need some help. You need lots of help.

J.—You can't help me.

Co.—M, what do you see he needs help in?

M.—He needs to learn how to keep his mouth shut, and he needs to learn how to act.

J.—I don't need no help from none of you. I don't want any help from anybody.

Co.—You don't want any help from any of us?

R.—That's his main problem. When somebody tries to help him, he won't let them. It is the same thing he was saying. If he won't help himself, how can we help?

J.—Be quiet. Oh, shut up, Peanut. Peanut, will you shut up! I'm leaving this group. I'm through with this group. This group can't help me. I don't like any of you, and I'm not gonna be in this group. I am through with them————, and I don't want anything to do with you or anybody in this group.

Co.—Sorry you feel that way, J. It sounds like we have been a little hard on you today. It seems like the boys had a lot on their minds.

H.—Yes, it is all true.

J.—I'm quitting. I don't want anything more to do with you. I don't want to come to any more of the group meetings. Count me out.

Co.—We'll leave it up to you, J. Whatever you decide is all right with us. I think though that we should leave it open if you would like to come back.

J.—I won't come back, and I won't have anymore to do with it.

M.—I hope you do come back, J. I like you. I just think there are some things you need to work on.

W.—Yeah, we like you, J. I'm sorry that you are so mad.

R.—I like you too, J., even if you are mad at me. And if you don't want to be in the group, I don't think you should have to be.

Meeting ends. J. says that he is quitting and is very angry. He comes back to counselor during the week, however, and apologizes for getting angry. He comes back to group and is a model group member.

SUMMARY

This chapter contains a review of the related literature and the development of a rationale for behavioral change of adolescents and preadolescents through activity group counseling. In addition, counselor and clients' roles are described, ground rules are given, the selection process is outlined, and the recommended size of an activity group is given.

Activity group counseling is an effective way of assisting the public school adolescents and preadolescents who have problems. Initial barriers to the establishment of good relationships essential for counseling are more easily overcome using activities as the vehicle by which therapeutic involvement can take place. Improvement in self-concept, relationships with others, and class-room behavior are outcomes that can be achieved through activity group counseling.

REFERENCES

Alexander, E. D.: School centered playtherapy program. *Personnel and Guidance Journal*, 1964, *43*, 256-261.

Allinsmith, W., and Goethals, G. W.: *The Role of School in Mental Health*. Joint Commission on Mental Illness and Health, Monograph Series No. 7, New York: Basic Books, 1962.

Axline, V. M.: *Play Therapy*. Boston: Houghton Mifflin, 1947.

Beard, J. H.; Goertzel, V., and Pearce, A. J.: The effects of activity group therapy with chronically regressed adult schizophrenics. *International Journal of Group Psychotherapy*, 1958, *19*, 38-40.

Blakeman, J. D.: The effects of activity group counseling on the self-evaluation and classroom behavior of adolescent behavior problem boys. Unpublished doctoral dissertation, University of Georgia, 1967.

Bonney, M. E.: *Mental Health in Education*. Boston: Allyn & Bacon, 1960.

Bonney, W. C.: Pressures toward conformity in group counseling. *Personnel and Guidance Journal*, 1965, *43*, 970-973.

Calia, V. F.: The culturally deprived client: A reformation of the counselor's role. *Journal of Counseling Psychology*, 1966, *13*, 100-106.

Carkhuff, R. R., and Berenson, B. G.: *Beyond Counseling and Therapy*. New York: Holt, Rinehart and Winston, 1967.

Clancy, N., and Smitter, F.: A study of emotionally disturbed children in Santa Barbara County Schools. *California Journal of Educational Research*, 1953, *5*, 209-218.

Coolidge, J. C., and Grunebaum, M. G.: Individual and group therapy of a latency age child. *International Journal of Group Psychotherapy*, 1964, *14*, 84-96.

Davids, M.: Integration of activity group therapy for a ten year old boy with casework service to the family. *International Journal of Group Psychotherapy*, 1955, *5*, 31-44.

Day, S. R.: The effects of activity group counseling on selected behavior characteristics of culturally disadvantaged Negro boys. Unpublished doctoral dissertation, University of Georgia, 1967.

Deutsch, M.: Minority group and class status as related to social and personality factors in scholastic achievement. New York: *The Society for Applied Anthropology*, 1960, Monograph No. 2.

Fiedler, F. E.: The concept of an ideal therapeutic relationship. *Journal of Consulting Psychology*, 1950, *14*, 239-245.

Fleischl, M. F.: The understanding and utilization of social and adjunctive therapies. *American Journal of Psychotherapy,* 1962, *16,* 255-265.

Foley, W. J., and Bonney, W. C.: A developmental model for counseling groups. *Personnel and Guidance Journal,* 1966, *44,* 576-580.

Gabriel, B.: An experiment in group treatment. *American Journal of Orthopsychiatry,* 1939, *9,* 146-170.

Galkin, J.: The possibilities offered by the summer camp as a supplement to the child guidance clinic. *American Journal of Orthopsychiatry,* 1937, *7,* 474-483.

Gazda, G. M.: New trends in counseling. *School Counselor,* 1965, *13,* 14-18.

Gendlin, E. T., and Beebe, J.: Experiential groups: Instructions for groups. In G. M. Gazda (Ed.): *Innovations to Group Psychotherapy.* Springfield, Ill.: Charles C Thomas, 1968, pp. 190-206.

Gibb, J. R., and Gibb, L. M.: Emergence therapy: The TORI process in an emergent group. In G. M. Gazda (Ed.): *Innovations to Group Psychotherapy.* Springfield, Ill.: Charles C Thomas, 1968. pp. 96-129.

Ginott, H. G.: *Group Psychotherapy with Children.* New York: McGraw-Hill, 1961.

Glasser, W.: *Reality Therapy: A New Approach to Psychiatry.* New York: Harper and Row, 1965.

Gordon, E. W.: Counseling socially disadvantaged children. In F. Riessman; J. Cohen, and A. Pearl (Eds.): *Mental Health of the Poor.* New York: The Free Press of Glencoe, 1964. pp. 275-282.

Gordon, E. W., and Wilkerson, D. A.: *Compensatory Education for the Disadvantaged.* New York: College Entrance Examination Board, 1966.

Gump, P., and Sutton-Smith, B.: Activity-setting and social interaction: A field study. *American Journal of Orthopsychiatry,* 1951, *1,* 311-318.

Jourard, S.: Invitations to being in therapy. Paper presented at the Annual Conference on Personality Theory and Counseling Practice, University of Florida, Gainesville, Florida, 1964.

Koenig, F. G.: A group therapy experiment in a city elementary school. *Understanding the Child,* 1949, *18,* 40-44.

Krumboltz, J. D., and Thoresen, C. E.: The effects of behavioral counseling in group and individual settings on information-seeking behavior. *Journal of Counseling Psychology,* 1964, *11,* 324-333.

Kvaraceus, W. C.: Education of the disadvantaged: Pretense or promise? Paper read at the Twentieth Teacher Education Conference, Athens, Georgia, 1967.

Landy, E., and Scanlan, E.: Relationship between school guidance and psychotherapy for adolescents. *American Journal of Orthopsychiatry,* 1962, *32,* 682-690.

Levy, D. M.: Outdoor group therapy with pre-adolescent boys. *Psychiatry,* 1950, *13,* 333-347.

Lieberman, F.: Transition from latency to prepuberty in girls: An activity group becomes an interview group. *International Journal of Group Psychotherapy*, 1964, *14*, 455-463.

Mink, O. T.: Education—the vision of America. *School Counselor*, 1966, *1*, 5-12.

Moreno, J. L.: *Psychodrama: The Principle of Spontaneity*. Vol. 1. New York: Beacon House, 1946.

Moustakas, C. E.: Emotional adjustment and the play therapy process. *Journal of Genetic Psychology*, 1955, *86*, 79-99.

Ohlsen, M. M.: *Guidance Services in the Modern School*. New York: Harcourt, Brace and World, 1964.

Olsen, J.: Challenge of the poor to the schools. *Phi Delta Kappan*, 1965, *17*, 79-84.

Patterson, C. H.: *Counseling and Psychotherapy: Theory and Practice*. New York: Harper and Row, 1959.

Patterson, C. H.: *Counseling and Guidance in Schools: A First Course*. New York: Harper and Row, 1962.

Patterson, C. H.: *Theories of Counseling and Psychotherapy*. New York: Harper and Row, 1966.

Patterson, C. H.: Psychotherapy in the school. In D. S. Arbuckle (Ed.): *Counseling and Psychotherapy: An Overview*. New York: McGraw-Hill, 1967, pp. 142-163.

Ramsey, G. V.: Sociotherapeutic camping for the mental ill. *Journal of Social Work*, 1964, 9, 45-53.

Riessman, F.: *The Culturally Deprived Child*. New York: Harper, 1962.

Rogers, C. R.: *Counseling and Psychotherapy*. Boston: Houghton Mifflin, 1942.

Rogers, C. R.: *Client-centered Therapy*. Boston: Houghton Mifflin, 1951.

Rogers, C. R.: The necessary and sufficient conditions of therapeutic personality change. *Journal of Consulting Psychology*, 1957, *21*, 95-103.

Rogers, C. R.: A tentative scale for the measurement of process in psychotherapy. In E. Rubenstein (Ed.): *Research in Psychotherapy*. Washington, D. C.: American Psychological Association, 1959. pp. 96-107.

Rorher, J. H.: Psychosocial development and acting-out behavior. In D. Schreiber (Ed.): *The School Dropout*. Washington, D. C.: National Education Association, 1964.

Rybach, W. S.: Disguised group therapy: An approach to the treatment of hospitalized teen-age patients. *Psychiatric Quarterly Supplement*, 1963, *37*, 44-45.

Shannon, P. D., and Snortum, J. R.: An activity group's role in intensive psychotherapy. *American Journal of Occupational Therapy*, 1965, *19*, 344-347.

Slack, C. W.: Experimenter-subject psychotherapy: A new method of introducing intensive office treatment for unreachable cases. *Mental Hygiene*, 1960, *44*, 238-256.

Slavson, S. R.: *Re-educating the Delinquent.* New York: Harper and Row, 1954.

Stranahan, M.; Schwartman, C., and Atkin, E.: Group treatment for emotionally delinquent boys and girls. *American Journal of Orthopsychiatry,* 1957, *27,* 518-527.

Tyler, L.: The method and process of appraisal and counseling. In A. S. Thompson and D. E. Super, (Eds): *The Professional Preparation of Counseling Psychologist.* New York: Bureau of publications, Teachers College, Columbia University, 1964, pp. 76-89.

Westman, W. C.: A troop of scouts. *Wisconsin Institute Discussion Paper,* No. 41, February 1963.

SUGGESTED READING

Axline, V. M.: *Play Therapy.* Boston: Houghton Mifflin, 1947.

Blakeman, J. D.: The effects of activity group counseling on the self-evaluation and classroom behavior of adolescent behavior problem boys. Unpublished doctoral dissertation, University of Georgia, 1967.

Day, S. R.: The effects of activity group counseling on selected behavior characteristics of culturally disadvantaged Negro boys. Unpublished doctoral dissertation, University of Georgia, 1967.

Ginott, H. G.: *Group Psychotherapy with Children.* New York: McGraw-Hill, 1961.

Moustakas, C. E.: *Psychotherapy with Children.* New York: Harper and Row, 1959.

Slavson, S. R.: *Re-educating the Delinquent.* New York: Harper and Row, 1954.

IV

A FRAMEWORK FOR GROUP COUNSELING[1]

Clarence A. Mahler

In the last ten years, group counseling has been expanding rapidly in both school and nonschool settings. The location of group counseling as a helping procedure between education on one hand and group therapy on the other hand has been a confusing situation. Working with a group in counseling resembles teaching much more closely than does counseling an individual.

The strong push toward individual counseling as the center of the guidance process may have been closely related to the desire for the young counseling profession to establish itself clearly apart from teaching. With increased maturity, jurisdictional disputes over professional boundaries become minor issues, and the issue of how individuals can be helped remains the central issue. On the other side, there has been the issue of counselors becoming sophisticated enough to be able to identify situations that might require intensive psychotherapy and to know when to refer for more extensive help. This issue arises clearly in differentiating the management of topics in group counseling as contrasted to their management in group therapy. The same topics do arise in class discussions, in group counseling, and in group therapy. The difference resides in how the leader handles the topic. The group counselor realizes that a series of ten to twenty group sessions is not usually sufficient to work out deeply involved personal conflicts and ambivalences.

So the group counselor settles for more reasonable and attainable goals, rather than extensive personality revision. How-

---

[1] This chapter is an abstracted version of Mahler's *Group Counseling in the Schools*. Boston: Houghton-Mifflin, 1969.

ever, for the leader to manage the group between mere class type discussion and deeply involved personal conflicts, he requires a philosophy of how people change as well as skills in aiding this process. This chapter aims to outline a point of view to help leaders establish a framework for working with groups and also review some of the crucial issues facing a group leader.

DEFINITION

Counseling can be viewed as a helping process aimed at aiding individuals to better understand their own and other people's behavior. The process may be concerned with a problem, with life patterns, and/or with identity seeking. Progress in counseling has been found to be closely related to the development of mutual respect, trust, and acceptance. Thus, it is important in aiding the client's growth and development that the counselor learn to be congruent, open, understanding, and accepting. In group, as well as in individual counseling, it is important that the client feels he is being understood, which means that the counselor and clients must listen perceptively and with understanding. Clients may not be able to explain themselves clearly, but they know immediately when they feel understood by the leader or group members.

Group counseling can be defined as the following:

> The process of using group interaction to facilitate deeper self understanding and self acceptance. There is a need for a climate of mutual respect and acceptance, so that individuals can loosen their defenses sufficiently to explore both the meaning of behavior and new ways of behaving. The concerns and problems encountered are centered in the developmental tasks of each member rather than on pathological blocks and distortions of reality.

The major concerns individuals bring to the group counseling center regarding the whole socialization process involve such questions as: How do youths become adults? Am I like other people or very different? Who am I, anyway? What do I really believe? How do I maintain a close relationship with my parents and yet establish my own individuality? What are my abilities and talents, and where can I use them? Do males and females really view the world differently?

Group counseling is a unique form of counseling; it is not group guidance nor is it group therapy. The former has tended to involve mainly the giving out of information and, in schools, is usually oriented toward encouraging students to know what the adults think the youngsters should know about themselves. Although the same topics may be discussed, the major responsibility in group guidance remains with the teacher. A group guidance unit on "How to Study" could be useful to a class in that information can be given and discussion of the topic can be useful to the students. However, in group counseling, the students initiate the discussion of concerns or problems. If the problem of studying arises, the leader and members strive to understand why the particular student is having trouble and also try to help him do something about it. The focus is upon the student, not the topic being discussed, and upon changing his behavior, not changing behavior in general.

It is important for the counselor to have a deep and thorough understanding of behavior, for example, being aware that there are multiple causes for ineffective study habits and numerous ways of making improvements in this area. The ability to time the use of the extensive knowledge and experience that a counselor brings to group counseling is both an art and a science. It is a science because he exposes his efforts and procedures to validation. It is an art because of the counselor's intuitive sensitivity for making an effective response, such as knowing when to make a suggestion, when and how to challenge a client to action, and when to support the client's efforts to face disturbing feelings.

Group counseling is, therefore, not group guidance, nor is it group psychotherapy. In group psychotherapy, there is more concern with unconscious motivation, and because of the depth of the growth problems faced by clients in group therapy, it is not unusual for the process to extend to many months and even years. The group counselor learns that he should not get into problems or situations that will take extensive time to understand and to manage. In a group counseling session, a student may raise a problem of how his parents have "grounded" him and penalized him severely for poor grades. Even though the counselor may be aware of severe emotional problems in the family, he must carefully guide the discussion so that it centers upon those aspects which the student and members of the group are capable of handling.

Problems encountered in group therapy often make it clear, for instance, that deep neurotic conflicts and attachments of a mother or father to a son or daughter are immobilizing a child and preventing him from doing good school work. Further, it should be obvious that helping these parents would be a long process. Thus, it is not so much that a counselor should be afraid of deep disturbance, but more that he should be realistic about what it takes to change behavior. One of the basic reasons for proposing group counseling programs is that group guidance does not sufficiently change behavior; but in the same regard, we should not expect group counseling to change deep-seated emotional and neurotic problems.

GOALS AND PURPOSES

A major goal of group counseling in schools is to build relationships that will enable the counselor to meet the important developmental needs of students, and to help with students' identity seeking process. Opportunities to learn more about oneself and to become more effective in one's own living and behavior can be provided.

Group counseling provides an opportunity for the students to examine in a friendly and permissive atmosphere their feelings, attitudes, and the ideas they have about themselves and the world. Each member of a group is encouraged to think for himself, to learn how to share his own perceptions, regardless of whether or not they are in agreement with those of other members of the group, and gradually he learns to accept responsibility for his own behavior. Members are encouraged to deepen their understanding of behavior and to learn not to be satisfied with a mere surface view of their own and other people's behavior. By being constantly alert, the counselor can reinforce statements and views of an individual which belong to him and actually represent his own ideas. It is important not to allow one person to speak for another, and in this way, each member is helped to respect the rights of other members, even when he disagrees with their point of view. Participating in a group project of this sort enables members to become more confident about their own abilities and skills; most members find that their tolerance and respect for others and for themselves increases immeasurably; they learn a deeper understanding of themselves as persons, and a greater skill in looking for possible alternatives in solving problems and crisis situations.

Students who have completed a group counseling experience seem to transfer their learning to later group interaction. In classes, they are more likely to speak up and give their own ideas of what they believe. Moreover, with the reinforcement of confidence in their own perceptions, they tend to meet the unexpected, as well as the expected, with a great deal more confidence and zest for living. Youths who gain a deeper understanding of behavior are not as likely to give ineffective and inadequate adults as bad a time as they may have previously. The insecure adults, however, may be disconcerted and upset by such youngsters when they have not learned to feel free in the expression of their own feelings and attitudes.

An understanding of the basic purpose of group counseling enables us to form a framework and helps counselors clarify their roles and functions. Group counseling is a method for accomplishing the following:

Exploring what it means to be a person: "Who am I, really?" "What do I want out of life?"

Developing greater confidence in one's own perceptions: "I know this is what I must do, even if my parents do not agree."

Learning to better understand other people; learning to really listen to others: "I can tune in to what people are saying, what they are really trying to express." "It amazes me that people can feel so differently about the same experience."

Integrating one's feelings and thinking: "I never thought about why Tim was behaving the way he did and I blew up. Now I can think things out." "I was afraid of anger and strong feelings, but I'm learning to handle them."

Becoming more effective in social situations: "I am not so afraid of meeting people and talking to them."

Reexamining one's present values and trying out new ones: "Always before I have just done what I thought my parents expected." "I realize that trying to please other people, to get their acceptance, really doesn't work very well."

Providing a safe climate for healthy exploration of feelings and control of them: "This is one place where we can say how we really feel." "I was so mad I could have killed him."

Learning how to be more responsible for one's own behavior: "I used to spend so much time fighting everyone, and not enough time knowing what I really wanted to do." "It's funny that pushing someone doesn't work, but still I have to learn how to influence others in order to get things done."

Exploring one's relations with other people such as authority figures, parents, teachers, siblings, peers: "I always wondered why people didn't seem to want me for a close friend, but now I am beginning to understand why." "It just had not occurred to me that I could get along better with my parents if I learned to understand them as persons, as well as being my parents."

Participation in group counseling can thus help people learn to be more natural, less defensive, more open to the richness of feelings, with an increasingly deeper capacity to enjoy living and experiencing. These reactions illustrate some of the main themes that have frequently shown up when people are asked what they have gotten out of a group counseling experience, although naturally there are wide variations among groups and among individuals within a particular group.

For the counselor, these basic purposes can provide a frame of reference and also give direction and purpose to his efforts. At times it seems as if some counselors are comparable to indecisive and insecure parents: they hope that their "permissiveness" will enable youths to find themselves. However, counselors must have a sense of purpose and direction or else they can accomplish very little, and they must use skill to enable their clients to benefit from the counseling experience. If a counselor's attitudes, such as "needing to save everyone" or "obtaining immediate signs and indications that he is of value," interfere with the process, then he should come to terms with his own attitudes and anxieties. He should face up to the anxieties that become manifested in his work, as well as be open to his own feelings, able to get feedback, and willing to work out the anxieties as a part of his own growth process.

A counselor is lacking in his knowledge and understanding of how behavior is changed if he is too eager to give answers, solutions to problems, and advice, instead of helping individuals discover answers and solutions for themselves. Furthermore, a counselor can frighten a group by "pushing a topic too fast" or by "insisting that everyone should talk," and also he is thereby falling down in his responsibility and use of proper timing. The counselor can learn a great deal about himself, and should not be afraid of making mistakes if he can learn from his mistakes, through the group counseling experience. Especially, he can be aware by obtaining feedback from the members of the group themselves or from listening to tapes of the sessions.

INDIVIDUAL COUNSELING AND GROUP COUNSELING

There has been a tendency among counselors to feel that group counseling is somehow in opposition to individual counseling, which, I hope I am making clear, is not true. Rather, we should assess the similarities and the differences between the two processes and see which areas are best handled by individual counseling, and in which areas group counseling seems to be the method indicated. Some of these areas can be easily identified, but much research is needed in order to determine the validity and ramifications of our clinical impressions. Until such research is carried out, we must utilize the clinical judgment of experienced counselors.

In the following areas, individual counseling appears to be the method indicated:

1. Solving a crisis problem that is very complicated, both as to causes and possible solutions.
2. When confidentiality is highly essential to protect the client and others.
3. Working through the meaning of test results in terms of one's self-concept. Individual tests can be utilized in groups, but they serve a limited purpose.

4. When fear of talking in a group is so great that the person does not seem to be able to get started in a group.
5. When an individual is grossly ineffective in relating to his peers and sets off such a strong immediate reaction that the group is more likely to be rejecting than accepting.
6. When a person's awareness and understanding of his own feelings, motivations, and patterns of behavior are very limited or so complicated that he feels lost and unable to share in a group.
7. Presents asocial behavior, particularly of a deviate nature.
8. When one's need for attention and recognition is too extreme to be managed in the group situation.

I do not wish to imply that these areas, problems, and situations should never come up in a group. Our main concern is to help the beginning counselor clarify his thinking about individual and group counseling, and to enable him to develop a frame of reference that will let him switch back and forth between the two processes according to the needs of his students or clients. Some counselors who are good in individual counseling find it difficult to be as proficient in group counseling, but it seems unlikely that the reverse would be true.

The primary value of group counseling seems to be in the following areas.

1. Learning to better understand a variety of other people, and finding out how others see things.
2. Learning a deeper respect for other people, particularly those who are different in many ways from oneself.
3. An opportunity to gain greater social skills in talking and relating to peers.
4. Learning to share with other people, especially an opportunity to gain a deeper sense of belonging from participation in a group in which one is a respected and accepted member.
5. A chance to talk about concerns, problems, values, and ideas with others who are facing similar situations.
6. Getting several people's reactions to one's problems and concerns.

7. Finding support from a group of peers, which is often of greater value to a student than support from an interested adult.
8. An opportunity for each person to spend more time with a counselor.
9. An opportunity to get involved rather slowly in the counseling process and to withdraw partially if a discussion becomes too threatening.
10. The counselor also has a chance to see clients in a broader and more active social setting than individual sessions provide.

The wide area of self-learning provided by a group counseling setting is often extremely beneficial to people and helps them particularly with the socialization process. One of the real values of group counseling over other types of group activity is the element of "controlled intimacy:" the group counselor helps each person share more deeply with others, but the initiation does not have to come from the individual, as it does in the development of friendships. The members of a group are helped to learn more about each other and yet are not obligated to continue the friendship pattern after or beyond the group sessions. A sorority or fraternity provides opportunites for social learning, but the pressures for conformity and loyalty are different from the group counseling experiences; also, it is possible to belong to social groups, such as fraternities, and yet never get to know other people very deeply.

Some of the areas in which individual and group counseling have more or less equal value are:

1. An opportunity to be accepted as a worthwhile individual.
2. Being responsible for one's own behavior.
3. Deepening the understanding one has of human behavior.
4. Being able to explore wider variations of one's emotional life and gaining greater confidence in the control of one's emotions.
5. Greater self-confidence and trust in one's own perceptions.
6. Gaining strength to be an individual in one's own right.

7. Examining one's interests and values and moving toward integrating them into a life plan.

It is evident that the major potentialities deriving from counseling are common in both individual and group counseling. By determining the purposes and needs of an individual requesting help and by designing the group counseling program to meet specific purposes, the counselor can provide valuable opportunities for members to learn and grow and live more effective lives.

THEORETICAL RATIONALE—IDENTITY SEEKING

The concept of ego-identity, or the idea of identity seeking, can provide the counselor with a foundation upon which to base his efforts to help clients, whether individually or in groups, in a school setting or other settings. Erik Erikson, in *Childhood and Society* (1963), should be credited with providing workers in the helping professions with a strong stimulus to recognize ego-identity as a significant concept. However, the term is not restricted just to Erikson's works, since much of what was called "self-concept" by George H. Mead and a "self-system" by Harry Stack Sullivan related closely to Erikson's use of the term ego-identity.

Robert White's book, *Lives in Progress* (1966), has a very helpful discussion of five growth trends that are characteristic of the normal process of growing up. These five developmental steps are related to the search for an identity and the ultimate goal of maturity and adulthood. Counselors will find it useful to study these five trends more extensively, although they will be listed here: (1) a trend toward a stabilization of ego-identity; (2) a trend toward freeing of personal relationships; (3) the deepening of interests; (4) humanizing of value; and (5) the expansion of caring.

Erikson sees the individual's growth and development in terms of eight stages, beginning with the earliest stage (in infancy) which he calls "basic trust versus mistrust." In early childhood the stage of "autonomy versus shame and doubt" gradually becomes "initiative versus guilt" and then "industry versus inferiority." Adolescence is the time of "identity versus identity diffusion."

It is during adolescence that the individual is most actively searching for and trying to define his identity, his place, and his role in life. The stages of adulthood are: "intimacy versus isolation and self-absorption," "generativity versus stagnation," and "integrity versus despair, and disgust."

Essential to Erikson's (1960) view of ego-identity is the combining of social and individual values.

> An increasing sense of identity is experienced preconsciously as a sense of psycho-social well-being. Its most obvious concomitants are a feeling of being at home in one's body, a sense of knowing where one is going, and an inner assuredness of anticipated recognition from those who count. Such a sense of identity, however, is never gained nor maintained once and for all. Like a "good conscience," it is constantly lost and regained, although more lasting and more economical methods of maintenance and restoration are evolved and fortified in late adolescence (p. 51).

The ego can be seen as essentially active, taking on or engaging objects in the environment, rather than passively absorbing experiences. Through active engagements and by confronting reality, the ego seeks to expand the individual's competence in dealing with reality; further, the ego guides and governs his actions in accordance with what is real. The organism responds, defends itself, and exhibits instinctual drives. But the ego is developing as the individual curiously explores his environment, attempts novel actions, and assesses the consequences of such actions. As the human being matures in his capacity to exercise perception, thinking, and motor control, his ego is able gradually to formulate and organize these processes in order to discover meanings and what is real (White, 1966).

In counseling, as well as in teaching and many other areas where "helping relationships" are to be fostered, we can be concerned about individuals' search for more of a sense of their own identity. Group counseling is one way for the counselor to exert a wider and broader influence on students and adults, one way he can make an important contribution to the identity-seeking process, especially during the school years. Indeed, identity seeking should probably be seen as one of the most basic purposes of education. The student's own experiences, his personal, unique ways of reacting are most certainly a significant part of the learning process. His need to develop self-understanding and more self-esteem is a vital part of this process, too. Furthermore, the school should contribute more to the socialization process through recognizing its role in developing students' social behavior, their ability to relate effectively with others, and their willingness to accept social responsibility.

Until recently, individuals could usually be expected to develop social competence and an ability to get along with others through their involvement in the total life of their families and communities. However, in our complex modern-day society, this development is seriously curtailed. Relatively few people have an opportunity to be truly a part of a natural, community-type group which initiates its own activities, provides the necessary leadership roles, and determines its own destiny. Thus, because families and communities are exerting less and less significant impact and direct influence on children, it becomes more and more the responsibility of schools to develop many kinds of preventive and remedial programs which will provide young people with the necessary ingredients for living effective and productive lives.

PLANNING FOR GROUP COUNSELING

Group counseling programs can be organized to meet a wide variety of needs and can have any number of purposes. The main consideration when organizing any group counseling program is to determine *For what purpose is this group being organized?* The stimulation to have a group may come from prospective members, from the counselor or school, from any social agency, or from one particular individual. Regardless of how the prospect of having a group arises, the focus should be on clarification of purposes. With a clear statement of purposes, the major facets of planning for a group tend to follow rather easily. Some of the major facets are as follows: size, frequency of meetings, duration of the life of the group, length of meeting time, setting for the meeting, open or closed groups, voluntary or involuntary participation, and preparation of members for group participation.

Variations in the major facets of group planning will reside mainly in the purposes giving rise to the idea of having a group. For example, a school may be considering having groups for their high school seniors. However, one can think of many possible purposes for having groups for high school seniors, some being: preparing for the years after high school, underachievement, discipline and behavior problems, married while in high school, sex as a meaningful part of life, socialization, and a chance to talk with one's peers.

Size

Research and practice indicate eight members as being perhaps the most frequent size group. The more difficult the problem or disturbed the members, the smaller the size is indicated. However, having five or less members adds the problem of too much homogeneity and increased pressure upon each member to talk. A group larger than eight provides a wider variety of personalities for each member to learn from, but reduces time available to each member as size increases.

Frequency of Meetings

Once a week for group counseling meetings seems to be a good average. One can then increase or decrease the frequency of sessions depending on the urgency and purposes of the group effort as well as on unavoidable circumstances surrounding the scheduling of meetings. It is possible to meet daily in group counseling sessions when basic purposes make it seem advisable. In one retraining program for the unemployed in New York City, an hour of group counseling was provided each day, along with three hours of job training and two hours of academic training. Even though there was considerable resistance among staff members to having this much counseling time, it soon became evident that without the daily group counseling sessions, the drop out rate would have increased greatly. Once-a-month meetings place great pressure upon participants to remember what transpired in the previous session and seem advisable only when there is no chance of more frequent meetings. Every-other-week meetings can sustain a group, but it takes a greater effort of involvement on the part of the leader to help bridge the time lapse between meetings. Various combinations of different frequencies could be explored. For example, it may be possible to begin a group with a marathon session and then go to an every-other-week meeting and still find that the progress is satisfactory.

Duration of the Life of the Group

Ordinarily, one should not think he has had a group counseling program unless the group has met for at least eight to ten times. The whole development of the group process and an understanding of how people change does not indicate that short contacts can be expected to have much impact on an individual's life. As one becomes a skilled leader, he will find his biggest problem in this area is that his group will not want to stop. In the school setting and many other agencies, there arise natural stopping points, such as summer vacations or semester breaks. The leader should give some thought to how long the group may go when he first begins to plan for his group. There is some research evidence to show that setting a limit on the number of sessions has a productive effect. At the present stage of our professional development, it seems advisable to set a time limit, allow a break of two or three weeks, and then allow members to return. If they all return, then the group goes on as it ended, if not, a new group begins.

Length of Meeting Time

Probably the most frequent length of meeting time is still the hour or class period. However, there is a developing tendency to have a wide variety in the length of a group meeting. Primarily this seems stimulated by the advent of marathon group counseling which may go up to eighteen to twenty-four hours and in some cases, even longer. In our experience of having over twenty different adolescent groups meeting on their own (out of school time), there was a strong tendency to have meetings of two or three hours once a week. Once again, the main purpose for the group meeting will help answer the question of the length of time for a meeting.

Setting For the Meeting

There is little research or literature on the effect of the setting on group performance. Ideally, a small room, nicely furnished, with provisions for privacy is indicated. However, in actual practice, we have had groups meet in an extremely wide variety of settings. To use tables or not is one of the early decisions a group leader must make. Tables provide a sense of security and a chance to hide one's legs. To be seated in a circle with no tables is to expose each individual much more to the whole group. Adolescents prefer a place where they can be informal and have privacy. When given a choice between meeting at school or a nonschool setting, they almost always select the nonschool setting.

Open or Closed Groups?

Beginning group leaders often find the question of open or closed membership rather bothersome. To have a closed group (with no new members added after the first few sessions) provides a much less complicated induction into the group. The advantages of having an open group are that any attrition can be made up by adding new members, and any imbalance in personalities can be restored by adding new members. In more informally organized groups, the members will often take full responsibility for bringing new members or for adding members when needed. The leader should give as much responsibility as possible to the group for making the decision to have an open or closed group. Advantages and disadvantages reside in both approaches, so careful consideration needs to be given.

Voluntary or Involuntary Participation?

The major goals of group counseling are more easily attained when members have a free choice in joining the group. The right to choose or not to choose to attend a group is the first step in giving the prospective group member responsibility for his own behavior. However, it is possible to go right ahead in certain situations, such as using all the trouble makers in a particular class or some other ready-made group as a complete counseling group. The leader must recognize that attendance is mandatory, and that he needs to be able to work with the members to clarify how group counseling may be of value to them. The procedures for getting members of an involuntary group involved are considerably different than the procedures used with voluntary groups. The leader must expect that a longer time will be needed to attain a working group; he can anticipate more testing of the leader and more resistance to becoming involved. Perhaps the only advantage of an involuntary group is the opportunity it affords the leader to demonstrate that he can handle hostility and resistance much more effectively than most other adults. In this very process of handling hostility and frustration, the leader may gain the respect and support of the members toward building a working group.

Preparation of Members for Group Participation

If at all possible, it is advisable to utilize the individual interview for inviting each potential member to join a counseling group. While it is possible to have a sign-up sheet and take members in a rather random manner, it aids the starting process to provide each member with an opportunity to discuss with the leader what may happen in the group and how he feels about joining a group. Where members recruit other individuals to join a group, it is important to give each new member an opportunity to tell the group why he wants to attend and what he has been told about the group as to what may happen in the group.

Ending a Group

The most opportune occasion to establish an ending time for a group is just before it begins. Very few successful groups want to end. So, it is helpful for the leader to anticipate the ending of a group and prepare for it right from the start. If a deadline or terminating date is not set early in the life of a group, it tends to be more difficult to arrive at a time when the whole group is willing to stop. Natural stopping places, such as the end of school or semester breaks, work well as stopping points.

STAGES IN GROUP DEVELOPMENT AND BASIC PRINCIPLES OF GROUP PROCESSES

In group counseling, it is helpful to focus on four different stages in group development: (1) the involvement stage; (2) the transition stage; (3) the working stage; and (4) the ending stage. The techniques used by the counselor and the principles underlying the group processes are somewhat different for each stage of development. The effective group leader needs to bring more than leadership skills to the group. He must have a frame of reference undergirding his whole counseling approach of how personalities grow and change. A part of this frame of reference comprises a group of basic principles that I have found most useful in helping individuals to live more meaningful lives. Other group leaders may have similar or additional principles that permeate their work, but it is highly important to have these operating principles clearly in view. The stages of group development will be reviewed first and then the principles will be presented.

THE INVOLVEMENT STAGE

Usually an individual joins a counseling group because he has certain needs and concerns. It is the main responsibility of the group leader to be able to take these individual needs and concerns and through the group process help them to be met. While there is much room for a leader to be quiet, there is no room for a leader to be passive and merely an observer. He should be listening closely to all presentation so as to know what the person may mean and how the presentation may help the individual and also the whole group.

Many individuals are unskilled in really getting to know another person or in sharing their own real selves. One of the underlying dynamics of why a group may accomplish closer relationships than an individual on his own resides in what I have called "controlled intimacy." To reach out to another person as a possible friend not only involves the fear of possible rejection, but the commitment of time and emotion that comes with close friendships. In group counseling this is taken care of because the leader sets the stage for sharing and getting to know each other. Members are not held responsible for direct commitments. They can feel and appreciate other people responding to them without worrying too much about being responsible. In fact, Berzon (1964) found that in leaderless therapeutic groups most members did not wish to take responsibility for their own deeper involvement in the group, nor did they wish to be held responsible for seeing that other members were helped to get involved.

During the involvement stage, a number of important tasks need to be completed to establish a working group.

Clarifying the Purposes

Regardless of how clear the purposes are for individuals to meet in a group, it is helpful to begin by reviewing why each individual wishes to be in the group. If the group is relatively clear about purposes, then the leader can go ahead with introductions and the warming-up process. If, on the other hand, there is a great deal of confusion and lack of clarity, the leader will need to spend more time clarifying purposes. The process of sharing one's reasons for being in a group helps to alert each member to his reasons and to allow for comparison with other group members. Some members may be alerted to other potentialities in the group other than the few they had already realized.

Further, the leader should be alert to the level of understanding as to why each member is attending. It is also possible for a member to want very much to be in a group and yet not be able to put his reasons into words. The best way to check the level of understanding as to why the group is meeting is for the group leader to write down his own reasons for having the group and then to check these against the reasons given by the members during the first session. With a reasonably good matching of the two views, the leader can feel free to proceed with the involvement process.

Getting Acquainted

The degree of structure in accomplishing the getting acquainted aspect is of minor importance. The real issue is to facilitate the early knowing of each member by the others and the setting of the initial steps in helping each member to deepen the *caring* part of his nature. While names carry much significance for us all, it is advisable to encourage members to give more than their names. I prefer not to structure too much what the persons should say about themselves since an open ended approach to having each person share provides the leader with much information on the level of sharing in which the group may engage, the degree to which the members are trusting of strangers, and many subtle clues as to how each group member goes about getting acquainted with strangers.

Beginning of a Trusting, Accepting Relationship

In addition to learning to trust the leader, members must learn to trust one another. For some people, this may be an entirely new experience since they may not have shared openly with people before. It will take such individuals some length of time before they can feel comfortable talking about their real feelings and their own behavior. The development of a basic sense of trust will vary greatly from group to group, and the leader should try to pace the group movement until this has been established. If the process of trust appears to be developing smoothly, the leader may proceed with the task of helping people learn how to change ineffective behavior and what it means to be a person. If, however, a trustful atmosphere is slow in developing, the leader will have to give special attention to this.

Beginning to Discuss Feelings and Behavior

As a part of the involvement process, the group counselor must encourage, reinforce, and help the members become able to express their real feelings. At the same time, he must help the members learn to respect one another.

To have the right to one's own feelings strongly supported in the group sets the stage for learning to be open, whereas disrespect of others—either overt or covert—inhibits the growth of trust and openness. The way a counselor handles the situations that arise, especially during the early discussions, will either confirm or deny the group's impression of him as an understanding and sensitive person whom they can trust.

Counseling is basically different from teaching in that the concern of the counselor is with the emotional reactions of the member to his present experiences as well as past experiences. Therefore, in group counseling, while the process of getting acquainted and clarifying purposes is going on, another whole process—the member's emotional response to the present experience—is going on simultaneously. The counselor must be aware of this and capable of handling both processes.

Principles Underlying the Group Process —Involvement Stage

There are certain basic principles underlying the group process. Some of these principles are particularly important during each stage and will be discussed in the appropriate sections. However, all of the principles in this stage are important throughout the four stages.

One Has a Right to His Own Feelings

In counseling it is important not only to help clients understand their own feelings and emotions but also to help them develop a respect for the rights of other people to have their own feelings, attitudes, and opinions. As a part of obtaining involvement, the group counselor must encourage and help members become able to express their real feelings. Frequently one member will try to tell another member how he should or should not feel about something. The counselor will try to help each member focus on how a person feels and not on whether he should or should not feel a certain way.

In reinforcing the right to one's own feelings, it is helpful to differentiate between feedback and criticism. Counselors are often confused when it comes to handling strong criticism or attacks from members of the group directed either toward people outside of the group or toward members in the group. When faced with strong criticism or outbreaks of hostility, the inexperienced counselor may want to (1) do nothing, or (2) quickly stop the criticism; whereas he should, by design, plan to use such outbreaks to help the members learn to manage hostility better. Each member needs to develop the ability to handle his own hostile feelings toward others as well as hostility directed towards him coming from other people. By using the term *feedback*, in place of *criticism*, the counselor can turn situations where a person is finding fault with someone into a positive view of getting feedback. This means getting reports from the group as to how each person is coming through to them, and finding out how they are receiving each person's efforts to communicate with them.

Each Individual Must Decide for Himself What He Will Work On

At times there is a tendency for some members of a group to pick out someone and urge him to talk and to work on his problems. This should be discouraged as much as possible by making it clear that each person is to decide for himself when and what he will work on. In any discussion, when an individual is being asked to look at his significant behavior or a difficult problem, it is important to get his assent and to let him decide whether or not he is ready for such a discussion. This principle also serves to discourage people in the group who want "to make someone else over." Along this same line, it should be made clear that each member has a right to be silent if he chooses. The leader or a member may call on a person to see if he wishes to contribute to the discussion, but if he does not want to, this feeling should be respected.

Each Individual Is to Work on Himself and Not on Others

By emphasizing that individuals are working on their own behavior, the leader helps the group avoid situations where criticism or complaints about other people serve to divert a person's attention away from himself. Thus, when a member brings up a problem he has with someone outside the group, he should be helped to see that it is *his* relationship with this other person and his reaction to the situation that is of primary concern. This principle also serves to reassure the significant persons in the lives of each group member that neither the leader nor the group members are centered on individuals outside the group. Group counseling does not stop with mere complaining about teachers, parents, spouses, or other nonpresent individuals. The process proceeds to helping the members present deal with whatever they are faced with in their own environment in as effective manner as possible.

How We Feel About a Situation Is the Crucial Point, Rather Than the Situation Itself

Group counseling sessions have little room for discussions, no matter how informative or interesting, that have no direct bearing on the behavior, feelings, and attitudes of the members themselves. Time and again the counselor will need to bring the group's attention away from general considerations and back to how the members feel about the topic being discussed. It is not the topic, per se, that is of concern to a group, but rather the persuading of each member to talk personally about whatever topic that is his concern. For example, a discussion on Viet Nam is appropriate in a group counseling session if it focuses on how the members present feel about Viet Nam. In the same way that the group does not work on individuals outside the group, it does not work on topics but on how group members feel about any topic. A good working group is one in which the members are able to take any statement of an individual's problem or situation and focus upon the real issues involved. Some members become very skillful in this kind of analysis and learn to give very accurate feedback to one another.

THE TRANSITION STAGE

This stage, while not easily delineated from the involvement stage and, in fact, beginning during the involvement stage, is important and predictable. It represents a position within the life of a group where all the steps and efforts for involvement have been conducted, and if successful, there is a readiness to move toward a commitment to use the group for one's own purposes. In the involvement stage, the leader is concerned that each member gets the opportunity to think through why he has joined the group, and at the same time, to check his expectations for the group against those of other members and the leader. The transition stage is a movement from procedures for accomplishing involvement to learning how to participate in a group effectively, both for one's own sake, and also to be of help to other members.

The beginning interactions and the development of relationships in a new group always produce some tension and anxiety. For some individuals, there will be considerable anxiety, particularly for those who have an underlying fear of not being responded to or fear of being rejected if they open themselves up. The less basic trust a person has—trust in himself, in people, and the world—the more cautiously he will approach real involvement in a group counseling experience.

The process of making a successful move from the opening stage to the transition stage depends to a great extent on the counselor's basic attitudes and his skill in managing the feelings of resistance and ambivalence in the members of the group. In a group, such as the self-selected high school seniors meeting on their own time, there is little to be concerned with in the transition stage. The involvement stage is rapidly accomplished, sometimes within one session. However, it is often necessary to be concerned with the group members' learning how to present themselves and how to incorporate into their group participation the basic principles of the involvement stage. As an example, one of the author's senior groups was invited to meet with an already established "academic discussion" group of very bright students. The group counseling members were able, in one session, to point out to this new group the difference between having a good discussion on world problems and the personalizing of their own discussion within a group.

The transition stage can best be managed by proper structuring and by the leader taking an active role during the early sessions. By the time the working stage is reached, the leader can relax considerably and then his role will be mainly that of a facilitator and summarizer. When the members have learned to work on their own problems and patterns and to recognize the meaning of their behavior, when they become willing and able to help each other, and when they develop a sense of responsibility to the group, then the leader's function in the working stage is much reduced over the involvement and transition stages.

Principles Underlying the Group Process
—Transition Stage

The basic principles underlying the group process are interdependent. While the principles are important at any stage of the group's life, the counselor must realize that certain types of behavior must be reinforced and definitely established before other types of behavior will be forthcoming. That is, it is difficult to establish the idea that *each individual must be responsible for his own behavior* until it has been made clear that *each individual must decide for himself what he will work on.* I long ago abandoned the idea of a counselor trying to be "neutral," since his values and ideas will be apparent. The more open he is about this, and the more openly and deeply he can share his values and the meaning life has for him, the more he will be able to stimulate the same process in his counselees.

There Are Many Advantages to Being Open

It is necessary for one to learn how to communicate his feelings and reactions to people who are close to him and significant in his life. Through self-disclosure, the purpose is not so much to help others understand a person, but rather to gain a deeper understanding of himself, as well as to learn more effective ways of behaving and relating to people. In group counseling, the sharing of feelings through self-disclosure and becoming more open is a very delicate process and requires a great deal of sensitivity on the part of the counselor. For some individuals in the group, trying to share feelings that they do not fully understand may produce anxiety. Also a person who tends to over-expose himself may need help in learning to go more slowly so as not to embarrass himself and others by premature self-disclosure. Learning to be more open and free in discussing one's feelings can lead to a fuller awareness of oneself. In a group counseling situation, each group member has an opportunity to tell about himself and find out how other people accept the picture he paints of himself. By learning to be open to feedback, which helps a person see the blind spots and ineffective behavior that he would not ordinarily be able to see, he can narrow the gap between his self-picture and the way he comes through to people. In adolescent groups, almost all of the groups go through a phase when each individual is given feedback regarding how he is perceived by every other member of the group.

People Can Better Understand Their Own Behavior

A group provides a good opportunity for people to become more aware of their deep feelings and also provides ways to learn to manage these feelings more effectively. Everyone has characteristic ways of facing the everyday world, and many of these reactions were learned far back in childhood. These "childhood residuals" are often detrimental to effective performance as adults, unless the adult can see how they are operating in his life. I often ask members in a group to look for their "childhood residuals." This gets individuals to see that reactions learned early in one's life are still being used indiscriminately in trying to cope with present-day situations. Reaction to authority is a very common residual. Also, the whole area of fears and anxieties can usually be seen in light of childhood residuals. Increased awareness and understanding of one's own behavior, both effective and ineffective, bring a feeling of stronger control and confidence in one's ability to handle life situations.

Each Is Responsible for His Own Behavior

One of the main tasks of counseling, and a task that group counseling is very well suited for, is to help each individual learn how to be more responsible for his own behavior and his own life. When a punitive, never-make-a-mistake climate exists in a home, or in a classroom, there is very little incentive for persons to respond to the idea of self-responsibility. Also, when responsibility is confused with conformity to social values, and when there exists in the present culture the deep ambivalence with regard to the idea of responsibility, one can perhaps see how large the task confronting counselors really is: "How do we help individuals accept self-responsibility?" The greatest help a group counselor can offer is to use every opportunity within the group to have the members take responsibility for what happens in and with the group.

THE WORKING STAGE

One of the real values of group counseling is the opportunity this type of situation provides for people to explore varied approaches to and alternative ways of solving problems. Once a group has reached the working stage (once a good working climate has been developed), most members will readily bring their problems to the group and will welcome help in making decisions or in better understanding things they are faced with.

By the time the working stage is reached, the leader's task is quite different from his task in earlier stages. By now the members have generally learned how to play this new social interaction game, and they have learned that it is mainly up to them as to what they will talk about. The idea of sharing fears, mistakes, or inadequate behavior is no longer so frightening. The right of each person to his own ideas, values, defenses, and feelings has been clearly established.

Usually the members of a group are eager to help each other, but they can be really helpful if they learn to understand the problem or concern in terms of the person who brings it up. Can they zero in; can they get to the crux of the matter? The leader can point out to the group wherein they have been helpful and effective in analyzing an individual's problem. Or if he feels that some members are being ineffective, he can point this out too.

Discussions of a member's ineffective behavior in the group should usually be in terms of asking the person to evaluate himself and then getting reactions from the rest of the group. In this way, feedback can be used to enable members to be aware of how they can help one another. Particularly, the leader should not be competitive or try to give "brilliant" insights and hypotheses. The real issue is whether or not the group is being effective in helping each other.

During the working stage, there is usually a high morale level and a definite feeling of belonging, so that the members feel that this is "their group." They may even wish to give the group a special name and may begin to tell friends about their group. Most members try hard not to miss a meeting and very often have learned to save up a situation or problem to be solved that they can share with the group. The members will have learned how to survey a problem carefully and to examine many possible causes before going on to discover possible solutions.

Principles Underlying the Group Process —Working Stage

The principles underlying the group process in the working stage are aimed at helping members actually change their ineffective behavior and attitudes. In group counseling, one is not content with allowing one to just enjoy the fellowship that the group provides; the basic purpose is to become more aware of behavior and to make specific and necessary changes.

Action Is Necessary to Change Behavior

There is a wide variation in members' abilities to put the learning opportunities of their group counseling experience into practice. One person is able to understand the concept of being responsible for his own behavior and takes steps which indicate that he has really learned this idea. Another may give lip service to this concept and not be able to carry through and actually do the things that he knows must be done. The group leader is alert to any cues that indicate that the members not only have a better understanding of their own behavior, but also have a desire to behave more effectively now and in the future.

In working with underachievers, for example, it is usually necessary to give them considerable help and encouragement to overcome their poor performance in school, particularly if the habit of underachievement is a long-standing one. Research studies have indicated that a minimum of two years of group counseling is usually needed before one can expect much change in the underachievement syndrome. This appears to be true because so much more of the total identity of the student is involved in this problem, over and beyond the fact of getting poor marks in school. Gently but firmly, the group leader and group members can encourage individuals in the group to take action. When the members are well aware that action is needed to change behavior, the leader can help them by supporting their efforts, while leaving to the individual the actual decision and timing for carrying out the action. The group should not concentrate on immediate success as the main goal, but rather on the development of skill and a willingness to face disagreeable tasks—a willingness to solve problems and resolve conflict situations.

Individuals Can Develop Alternatives for Meeting Difficult Situations

In addition to gaining skill in analyzing conflicts, problems, and patterns of behavior, members can be helped to learn more creative ways of visualizing alternatives that are open to them. Quite often when a member expresses his fears, he can be challenged to face the very problem that is confronting him: "Yes, and what if you fail biology, then what will happen?" If your parents do go ahead and get a divorce, then what?" "Your parents want you to finish college before getting married, whereas you want to get married sooner than that; what are the various alternatives open to you?" By challenging people in this way, the counselor is saying to them, in effect: "Supposing what you are afraid of happens. Do you not have sufficient inner resources, and can you not just face the difficult situation? What kind of strategies can you develop within yourself to help meet any problem or predicament you may encounter?"

A Commitment to Change Is Very Helpful

The leader should be aware when members of his group seem to be having difficulty in translating the discussion ideas and insights into action, or in making these ideas meaningful in their own lives. Very often it helps to talk to these members individually. In an individual session, the counselor and member can explore possible reasons for the lack of commitment to the purposes of the group. The counselor can also watch for attempts, no matter how small or tentative, on the part of members to take action and to make meaningful changes in their lives. He can encourage and reinforce these attempts whenever possible.

THE ENDING STAGE

Whenever a group has developed a deep, meaningful, caring relationship, the members are very reluctant to see this come to an end. Most people find it deeply satisfying to be part of a group and to have a place where they can freely express their feelings, fears, anxieties, frustrations, hostilities, ideas, aspirations, and anything that really concerns them. Our present society seems to offer few opportunities for real and satisfying relationships of this sort. Indeed, a very important aim of group counseling is to demonstrate that close, caring relationships are possible. And the counselor's wish is that, as a result of the group experience, members will learn how to develop real relationships with people in the significant areas of their lives, particularly in the areas of home and work. Possibly former members of a counseling group will want to participate in other types of group programs; they should be encouraged to look for ways to help organize and lead group sessions in their school community, church, or work after they "graduate" from the group counseling program.

The ending stage can be seen as a "commencement" in that the counselor and members are thinking in terms of how to apply what they have learned to the future and further development of their lives. Discussion with the group concerning how everyone feels about the approaching termination of the sessions is very important. A counselor working with high school students will realize that it is almost inevitable for these students to feel a sense of rejection when the group is ending. They can easily interpret the termination of a group, to which they have become very attached, as one further indication that adults will "always let them down" and are not to be trusted. It is helpful to present the idea that relationships may ease but that the caring that has developed does not need to stop. Also, caring is a way of living that helps one to expand and live a more meaningful life, rather than be hurt by breaks in relationships.

Principles Underlying the Group Process
—Ending Stage

Members Can Put Their New Learnings Into Practice in Their Daily Lives

How do clients transfer effectively into their lives what they have learned during group counseling sessions? Mainly this transfer can be facilitated if the leader has emphasized all along the importance of taking action and making changes in attitudes and behavior. During the working stage, there should have been numerous opportunities for members to learn such things as being more assertive and self-confident, being more aware of their real feelings, controlling their emotions, and recognizing how attitudes of hostility affect their interpersonal relationships. The counselor may ask his group at some time during the last two or three sessions "What aspects of your personality and behavior do you propose to work on during the next year, or during the next five or ten years?" "What impact have the things we have been discussing had on your life?" Reviewing and clarifying the group's experiences as part of the ending stage can help members see ways in which they can keep on learning and growing in future years.

Becoming More Deeply Aware and More Accepting of Oneself Is to Become Less Defensive

The principles mentioned earlier, which concerned the value of learning openness to one's feelings, were applicable mainly to what was happening during the group sessions. But gradually the counselor should utilize the meaningful experiences of the group to suggest ways in which the members might transfer these experiences to their day-to-day behavior. One strong indication that people are learning to be open is when they appear to be less defensive, when they have less fear of rejection, and are less sensitive to criticism.

When people see that they can be more open to their own feelings and more accepting of themselves, they develop more self-confidence and more of a sense of their own identity. This does not happen automatically but is a process that can be fostered and nurtured by an understanding counselor. The group counseling relationship is an ideal place to learn how to accept oneself—one's strengths as well as weaknesses. Learning to be open to feedback and evaluation from others, learning "to see ourselves as others see us," is a very important outcome of group counseling.

SUMMARY

Group counseling has been a rapidly expanding field in the last ten years, both in school and nonschool settings. Group counseling is viewed as a field that comes midway between group guidance on one hand and group therapy on the other. The major concerns that arise in group counseling programs center around the socialization process; thus the deeper involvements of neurotic and psychotic behaviors are avoided. Group counseling differs from group guidance in not being preplanned as to topics and also dealing much more, than in group guidance, with the feelings of the group members.

Group counseling provides an opportunity for the members to examine their feelings, attitudes, and behaviors and compare them with their peers. The program encourages members to learn how to examine a problem, to understand a difficult situation, and still come up with possible solutions. Strong support is given to the development of one's own values and confidence in managing one's own life.

Individual and group counseling are not seen as competing systems. Rather, there is a need for both individual and group counseling, often with the same members. The problem and situation an individual is faced with goes a long way toward determining if he needs individual sessions or group sessions or both. A counselor must be able to do both kinds of counseling, or rather, it is hard to conceive of a group counselor that is not a good individual counselor. Some counselors, however, may not be as capable in group work as they are in individual counseling.

The concept of identity seeking, based on the work of Erikson, provides a theoretical foundation for the counselor on which to base his work. Other views may serve as a guide for the group counselor, but certainly some viewpoint is deeply needed.

The strongest guide in helping organize a new counseling group is a clear delineation of the purpose for having the group. When the purposes are clearly stated, the group leader then has little trouble deciding on the size of the group, how frequently to meet, how long the group will meet, how long to meet at each session, where to hold the meetings, to have a closed or open group, and the like.

Four stages of development are proposed for the group processes that occur in the life of a group. These are the involvement stage, the transition stage, the working stage, and the ending stage. The techniques used by the counselor and the principles underlying the group processes are somewhat different for each stage of development. The involvement stage is centered on the task of facilitating the involvement of each group member and beginning an atmosphere of trust and acceptance that will enable members to work more effectively. The transition stage is a crucial one of moving from opening exercises to a commitment to work on oneself. The working stage is accomplished when the group members have learned how to present themselves effectively to the group and the group has learned how to skillfully help members work through problems and situations. The ending stage is concerned with using the end of the group to further more effective living in the future.

Twelve basic principles are presented in a somewhat hierarchical sequence to go along with the stages of group development. These principles are presented to help the group leader focus on some of the underlying learnings that go on in a group and to help him facilitate their being learned by the group members.

REFERENCES

Berzon, B.: The dimensions of interpersonal responsibility in therapeutic groups. Mimeographed report No. 1-No. 3, *The Intensive Group Experience.* San Diego: Western Behavioral Sciences Institute, 1964.

Erikson, E. H.: Identity and the life cycle. *Psychological Issues,* 1960, *1,* (1, Whole No. 1).

Erikson, E. H.: *Childhood and Society.* New York: Norton, 1963.

White, R. W.: *Lives in Progress.* New York: Holt, Rinehart, and Winston, 1966.

SUGGESTED READING

Bonney, W., and Foley, W.: The transition stage in group counseling in terms of congruence theory. *Journal of Counseling Psychology,* 1963, *10,* 136-138.

Cohn, B. (Ed.): Guidelines for Future Research on Group Counseling in the Public School Setting. Cooperative Research Project No. F-029—Research Seminar on Group Counseling, Board of Cooperative Educational Services, Bedford Hills, New York, 1964.

Gazda, G. M.; Duncan, J. A., and Meadows, M. E.: Group counseling and group procedures—Report of a survey. *Counselor Education and Supervision,* 1967, *6,* 305-310.

Hummel, R. C.: Ego-counseling in guidance: Concept and method. *Harvard Educational Review,* 1962, *32,* 463-482.

Samler, J.: Change in values: A goal in counseling. *Journal of Counseling Psychology,* 1960, 7, 32-39.

Shlien, J. M.; Mosak, H. H., and Dreikurs, R.: Effect of time limits: A comparison of two psychotherapies. *Journal of Counseling Psychology,* 1962, *9,* 31-34.

Spieler, F. R., and Biancovisco, A. N.: The hundred hour challenge: Group counseling in a manpower development training program. Mimeographed report, 1965.

V

BEHAVIORAL GROUP COUNSELING

BARBARA B. VARENHORST

T HE NUMEROUS TERMS which have been given to a maturing theory of counseling aid in the understanding of the significant concepts contained within the theory. Whether the terms used are "behavioral counseling," "behavior modification," "behavioral therapy," "social learning," or "reinforcement learning," attention is called to prime words such as "behavior" and "learning" and a principle of learning, i.e., "reinforcement." In simple and general terms, the theory of behavioral counseling states that most human behavior is learned. Such learned behavior is acquired as well as maintained or modified through the principles of respondent and operant conditioning, reinforcement, observational learning (modeling), generalization, and discrimination. The fact that this theory emphasizes observable behavior is not its unique characteristic. The objective of *all* guidance, *all* education, and *all* teaching is to affect behavior. In fact, the only *evidence* of learning is a change in behavior, since behavior is the only criterion against which to measure learning. In this sense there is no such thing as "nonbehavioral" guidance, or counseling, or teaching. The theory is unique or revolutionary as Krumboltz (1966) has indicated because knowledge of the learning process is leading to the development and use of specific counseling procedures or techniques for changing behavior. Such changes in behavior can be observed and therefore evaluated.

For years, psychologists engaged in clinical treatment of clients have utilized principles of learning in their therapy practices. Some of these psychologists have subsequently used learning principles to explain, after the fact, what took place in therapy (Dollard and Miller, 1950). Behavior counseling or

119

therapy *starts* with concepts of learning and develops a program for behavior change based on these concepts. Such programs are designed specifically for a *particular* individual, *group* of individuals, or *particular* problems. The principles themselves give direction to specific techniques that can be used in therapy *before* counseling or therapy is begun.

Behavior counseling focuses on behavior that can be defined and observed, ". . . those activities of an organism that can be observed by another organism or by an experimenter's instruments" (Hilgard, 1962, p. 614). This aspect of the theory is of utmost importance to the counselor who would ask the following questions: (a) What behavior in the student should be decreased, and what behavior should be increased? (b) What variables (changing characteristics) in the environment are currently maintaining this behavior? What variables are inadequate which inhibit the desirable behavior from being performed? and (c) What resources, or environmental elements are available for altering the student's behavior? When behavior is viewed as that which results from acquiring an association between an environmental stimulus and some human response, then all behavior, whether adaptive or maladaptive, can be seen as changed or maintained by the same principles of learning. To clarify, the following example is given.

A child may find that when he throws a temper tantrum (an individual response), his mother picks him up and comforts him (an environmental stimulus). If the mother wishes her son to stop his tantrum behavior, she must (1) refrain from picking him up or attending to him when he has the tantrum and (2) provide the attention and comfort he wants when he is doing something she wants him to do, i.e., playing quietly by himself, or show him alternative, but acceptable ways of getting what he wants.

THEORETICAL PRINCIPLES

Ullmann and Krasner (1965) have said, "Despite differences in approaches and techniques, we would propose that all behavior modification boils down to procedures utilizing *systematic environmental contingencies to alter the subject's response to stimuli*" (p. 29). This can be restated as procedures that use systematic events or occurrences in the environment to change the client or student's reactions to what happens to him. For example, the client tells the therapist that he is totally inadequate and incompetent. The therapist replies with denial, assuring the client that he *is* adequate and competent in certain areas. An environmental contingency has been established which may lead to an increased number of self-degrading comments by the client. To alter this, and to encourage self-constructive comments from the client, the counselor must systematically refrain from responding to the self-degrading comments of the client, if the objective of therapy is to reduce self-degrading behavior, or increase the extent to which a client speaks highly of himself.

Ullmann and Krasner (1965) go on to point out that the systematic or programmatic arrangement of the environment as well as the response to stimuli are crucial to a treatment program. It is not sufficient to merely "remove" maladaptive behavior in a person's responses. This maladaptive behavior should be replaced with a more adjustive behavior, which is incompatible with the previous behavior, if the modification is to be maintained.

The principles of the theory are based in a large part on B. F. Skinner's early work on operant conditioning (1953), and on the principles of classical conditioning introduced by I. P. Pavlov (1927) in the 1920's. Greenspoon (1962) and Krasner (1955), among others, did early research to investigate operant conditioning principles. The basic principles of classical conditioning have been elaborated upon by Hull (1943) and Wolpe (1958, 1962). Operant conditioning requires that a person do something (operate on the environment) which produces an event or response and which eventually may come to be associated with performing that behavior, i.e., the baby cries, the mother picks him up. Crying becomes conditioned to being picked up. Classical, or respondent conditioning states that the stimulus must be given first, following which a response is elicited. A bright light (stimulus) is beamed into a person's eye. Immediately the eye blinks. Such responses can be paired or associated with neutral stimuli which when so done will cause the same response to occur. An eye blink is paired with certain music by presenting the music at the same time the light is used. Eventually the music alone will produce the eye blink.

Reinforcement

Conditioning is the term used to describe the process by which behaviors and events, or stimuli, are paired to the point where the stimulus is a prerequisite for the behavior to occur. The pairing is established by the subject's reaction to the stimulus which is associated with the behavior he has performed. If in response to a stimulus, a behavior is increased, then one would conclude that the stimulus is a reinforcing stimulus. If the stimulus does not affect the frequency of the occurrence of a behavior, then one would conclude that it is *not* a reinforcing stimulus. "It is crucial to state explicitly that frequency of emitted behavior is the prime operational definition of reinforcing stimuli . . ." (Ullmann and Krasner, 1965, p. 17). Respondent behavior is an involuntary human response to a stimulus. (The eye tears in response to peeling onions.) Operant behavior is a voluntary human response operating on the environment in degree, kind, and frequency depending on what has happened and is happening following that behavior. (The child eats his meat and vegetables and is given the ice cream he wants.) Two types of reinforcement affect the frequency of these responses: positive and negative.

Positive reinforcement is defined as the presentation of stimuli that act to *strengthen* the behavior that they follow due to the fact that those stimuli are highly valued by the person. Usual examples of positive reinforcers are candy, money, smiles, and praise which are presented to a person following emitting behaviors.

Negative reinforcement is the presentation of stimuli that strengthen responses through their *removal*, in which case the subject is reinforced for his behavior of getting rid of stimulation. An example of this would be closing one's eyes or covering one's ears to cut out glaring lights or piercing sounds. The closing of one's eyes is increased in frequency because it eliminates a light that is unpleasant to the person. Going to sleep may be reinforced if it eliminates having to listen to a nagging parent. It can be said, then, that a negatively reinforcing stimulus is one that strengthens the response that takes it away.

The concept of reinforcement in affecting behavior is a crucial principle in behavioral counseling and one that should be thoroughly understood by one doing behavioral counseling. Difficulties related to its use will be discussed later in this chapter.

Extinction

The process by which a person may rid himself of an already-conditioned behavior, or how he learns not to do something is called "extinction." This is accomplished by the withholding of reinforcement. The example of the temper tantrum illustrates this concept. The mother, wishing to eliminate tantrum behavior, withholds attention following a tantrum. She may find that instead of a cessation of the tantrum, the child may display even more violent temper, expecting eventually to get what he wants. Frequently he does because the mother cannot stand the additional torrent of acts. If the mother can refrain over long periods of time from attending to such behavior, she may eventually extinguish it when the child wants her attention. To completely rid the child of such acts, she may need to demonstrate other acceptable ways of getting her attention.

The extent to which a person is successful in extinguishing behavior is highly dependent on schedules of reinforcement used during the training of the behavior. If every response has been reinforced, extinction may be achieved rapidly. Intermittent reinforcement, however, leads to greater resistance to extinction, since the person will persist in that behavior, expecting eventually to be reinforced. Many human behaviors have been acquired through random schedules of reinforcement, since reinforcement frequently is unsystematically administered and may come from a variety of sources. To extinguish such behaviors requires a careful study of the sources and patterns of reinforcement maintaining them.

Generalization

When a behavior becomes conditioned to a response or

stimulus, other similar stimuli will also produce this behavior. This is called "generalization," which is a reaction to novel situations in accordance with their degree of similarity to familiar ones. The amount of generalization decreases as the second stimulus becomes less similar to the original conditioned stimulus. A child is criticized by a parent for wearing certain clothes. Although he persists in wearing these clothes, he avoids the presence of his parents as much as possible. If he is also criticized for his apparel by his teachers, anticipation of criticism may "generalize" to all adults with the subsequent avoidance behavior of all adults. This would be an example of generalization that can take place in learning.

Discrimination

If the same boy experiences acceptance or approval of his clothes by some adults, such as a counselor, he may learn "discrimination." Discrimination is critical to learning if a person is to be able to refine or adapt his behavior to differing demands and situations. A person who is unable to discriminate, with respect to his behavior, may frequently fail to get the kind of reinforcement he wants. This may lead to a kind of maladaptive behavior requiring therapy or counseling. Simply stated, discrimination is the giving of reinforcement in the presence of one stimulus and withholding it in the presence of another. Conditioned discrimination is brought about through selective reinforcement and extinction so that of two stimuli similar to each other, the one reinforced will elicit the behavior while the one ignored will extinguish the behavior. Often, training in discrimination is necessary in order to bring about more adaptive behavior.

Desensitization

The learning principles that have previously been discussed have primarily dealt with operant conditioning, or the voluntary behavior associated with environmental contingencies. In the course of living, many people acquire involuntary behavior, or respondent learning associated with events or objects. Such examples might be the tightening of the stomach muscles or shortness of breath before getting up before an audience to give a speech, or quickened heart beat, dizziness, and perspiration when standing on some high place, or autonomic fear responses when passing a school or university where unpleasant experiences may have occurred. Ullmann and Krasner (1965) identify this type of responding in accordance with Hull's theory of learning, "Where Skinner's concepts are based on the frequency of emission of overt behaviors, Hull distinguishes between performance, the overt behavior, and habit, the modification of the central nervous system, which mediates learning and which is not directly measurable" (p. 18.). They go on to explain that, according to Hull, a performance is the product of habit strength and drives, such as hunger or thirst, and that some of these habits or drives must be inhibited by natural means, such as rest and relaxation, and other habits, must be inhibited by counter-conditioning. Thus these two authors credit Hull's theory as the basis for Wolpe's systematic desensitization procedure in which a conditioned drive (anxiety) may be inhibited by associating the appropriate stimulus (speech giving) with an image or other cue (relaxation) which is incompatible with an anxiety response. This concept has been shown to be very effective by Lazarus (1963) and Wolpe (1958, 1961) in modifying maladaptive behavior.

Observational Learning: Modeling

It has been shown that through the application of the learning principles that have been discussed, behavior can be increased, altered, and maintained by counselors or therapists. Such principles, however, are primarily useful in affecting behavior that is already contained in the person's repertoire of skills or behavior. An individual must perform a behavior before it can be reinforced. Some maladaptive behavior is due to the fact that the person simply does not have this behavior in his repertoire; he does not know how to perform the appropriate behavior for which he may earn positive reinforcement. This, then, is a problem of acquiring or learning new behaviors.

Bandura has debated this issue in relationship to the concept of modeling (Krasner and Ullmann, 1965). He makes an important distinction between what he calls performance and learning.

Operant conditioning is an exceedingly reliable and efficient method for strengthening and maintaining responses that already exist in the behavioral repertoire of an organism. Through careful management of incentives, the frequency, amplitude, latency and the discriminative patterning of responses can be readily modified. Most of the psychotherapeutic applications of this principle have, in fact, been concerned with problems of performance rather than of learning (p. 313).

He goes on to say that while conditioning methods are well suited for controlling existing responses, they are often exceedingly laborious and inefficient for developing new behavioral repertoires. Further, much social learning is fostered by exposure to real-life models who perform, intentionally or unwittingly, patterns of behavior that may be imitated by others. He argues that it is far more efficient to use a skilled model to demonstrate correct responses in their appropriate sequence, or a symbolic model presented pictorially or through verbal descriptions than it is to reinforce in successive steps random trials of behavior. At times, this successive approximation method could even be dangerous or fatal, since a person might not have a second chance to try again.

The effectiveness of this learning technique has been demonstrated in numerous experiments that Bandura and others have conducted. It is, therefore, an important technique to be used in individual and group counseling. Although many aspects of the concept still need more extensive and careful study, such as variables attending the effectiveness of models, the prestige of the models, the emotional condition of the person observing the models, and negative consequences of modeling, enough is known at the present time to qualify it as a pertinent learning concept for counseling techniques.

APPLICATION OF THEORY TO THE COUNSELING PROCESS

Numerous applications of these learning principles to clinical treatment problems have been made by therapists and psychologists. The reader is referred to Ullmann and Krasner (1965) *Case Studies in Behavior Modification* and to Krasner and Ullmann (1965) *Research in Behavior Modification* for specific examples. Such problems as school phobias, enuresis, tantrum behavior, thumb sucking, tics, stuttering, schizophrenia, and autism have been successfully treated (using behavior modification techniques) with lasting results and without symptom substitution. In the past few years, serious attention has been given to the counselor's application of such techniques in normal school settings. Such applications should be of greatest interest to school counselors engaged in group counseling.

When one reflects on the learning principles that have been discussed, one recognizes how common-place these concepts are and how they are operating continually in all facets of people's lives. People are constantly being taught by others as they interact in social situations, and people learn from experiences that happen to them, whether this learning be consciously or unconsciously acknowledged. One's subsequent behavior reflects the learning that has taken place. On the other hand, most people unwittingly are manipulating the behavior of others by what they do or do not do in response to them. The process goes on even when it is not systematically planned or controlled. Problems arise, however, because much of what we do to others *is* unsystematic and random. Even intentional acts meant to bring about more desirable behavior in others react in reverse, much to the frustration and frequent anger of those who would control behavior. When this occurs, correcting the situation or modifying the behavior requires careful analysis in order to understand the variables maintaining the behavior so that new or different responses might be substituted. Specific examples from a school environment may clarify this point.

It is commonly assumed that attention is a reinforcer of behavior, i.e., attending to a behavior increases the frequency of occurrence of that behavior. It is important to recognize that although positive attention in the form of praise and smiles is probably the preferred type of attention, negative attention (such as criticism, sarcasm, and nagging) also tends to increase the frequency of occurrence of the behavior. They, too, are reinforcers. It is frequently said that negative attention is far more preferable than rejection or being ignored. In a classroom situation, a poor student who gets the D's and F's on papers, never receiving praise or compliments, and whose hand may be ignored because the answer is never right may find that the teacher *does* attend to him when he talks to his neighbor, comes in late, or is a general disturbance in class. Such attention will undoubtedly be of the negative type, but nevertheless, he *is* someone and this may be important to him. This attention may generalize to all teachers in the school and include counselors, deans, and even the principal. On reflection, one is aware that one can usually remember the real trouble makers who went through the school even after the very good student has been forgotten. That person has made his place in the memory and history of the school.

In the author's experience there was a Johnny who will never be forgotten and who was a skilled behavioral engineer with respect to manipulating the adults throughout the school and his home. He did not have the skill or social competence to be successful in our school. He could not read more than on a second-grade level, nor write a complete sentence without errors. His attention span or level of concentration was that of an elementary school child. He had failed subject after subject and was still a tenth grader at age 18. Johnny found that by coming late to class, failing to turn in papers, being absent from school, having frequent headaches or stomach aches all had rewarding consequences. The counselor frequently called him in for conferences, teachers had case conferences on him, the dean called him in and sometimes held conferences at school with him and his mother. These conferences meant that his mother had to take time off from work to come, which resulted in much "attention" that night at home. The nurse was involved in attending to him and even the principal recognized him and was aware of him. The vicious cycle of reinforcing maladaptive behavior had been set in motion, and it was extremely difficult to know how to break into the cycle to reverse the process and change the behavior.

Another example of the unprogrammatic aspect of maintaining and encouraging undesirable behavior is contained within the philosophy and operation of the guidance program itself. Many students are not "special" to any one adult in our society today. Mother and father, if present in the home, may be very busy and involved in their own work, concerns, and responsibilities. Little time is left over for attending to each child in the home. Teachers are concerned with groups of students and seldom recognize or convey specific interest in one particular student. How then does a child get the attention that he desires? Counselors are available for helping students with "problems" and frequently are so overloaded in dealing with students with problems that little time is left over to see those without "problems." However, if one does develop a severe enough problem he may get to see his counselor and receive some attention. Consequently, the guidance staff may unwittingly be encouraging the development and maintenance of problem behavior, rather than alleviating it according to design. This is a sobering thought. Problems seem to require attention. To counteract this, plans could possibly be made to provide for success, attention, and recognition through acceptable ways, which would be incompatible with the less desirable behavior and which would be strengthened by the positive reinforcement that would follow such behavior.

Perhaps these examples have demonstrated the point that principles of learning should be recognized and can be applied to techniques and methods not only to modify behavior that is unproductive or undesirable but also to the planning of the desirable development and learning for all individuals in school and society. These principles have relevancy not just for the counselor and his guidance program, but for the teacher in her classroom and the principal and curriculum director in the planning of educational experiences and activities.

RATIONALE FOR BEHAVIORAL GROUP COUNSELING

From an increasing body of experimental data based on studies done by Krumboltz and others at Stanford University, it is being demonstrated that the learning principles previously discussed can be translated into extremely effective counseling techniques. In three earlier studies done by Krumboltz and Schroeder (1965), Krumboltz and Thoresen (1964), and Ryan and Krumboltz (1964), it was clearly shown that student behavior can be significantly affected by counselor reinforcing statements. It was also demonstrated that the increase in criterion behaviors within the counseling setting did generalize to behavior after leaving the counseling interviews. Students did engage in significantly more information-seeking activities, decision-making and deliberation-making behaviors in other neutral settings than did those students who did not receive reinforcement counseling. Students used in these studies had volunteered for special vocational or educational counseling, which provided the experimenter with a natural counseling situation rather than a contrived one.

Other studies examined not only the effect of reinforcement counseling, but some type of modeling procedure on the behavior of students. The Krumboltz and Schroeder study (1965) and the Krumboltz and Thoresen study (1964) both used a 15-minute tape recording of a high school boy who was engaged in seeking information relevant to his educational and vocational plans. Thoresen, Krumboltz, and Varenhorst (1967) extended these studies to investigate the model characteristic of sex. On one tape, a female counselor with a male student was used; on another, a "male counselor, male student" combination was used. Four such combinations were applied in the experiment. This was done because the earlier studies found that, although the audio-model was significantly effective in affecting the behavior of boys, it was not as effective with respect to females. The latter study found that model reinforcement procedures were, on the average, more effective than control procedures for males but not for females; that male students responded best when males were all in other roles; and that female students responded best when a male counselor presented either an all-male or an all-female model tape.

Bruner (1965) found that programmed instruction and other forms of written material can serve as effective models for producing desired behavior with high school students, and Krumboltz, Varenhorst, and Thoresen (1967) found that video-taped presentations are effective in influencing the information-seeking behavior of female high-school students.

It seems reasonable that if these techniques have been shown to be useful in eliciting a greater frequency of certain types of behaviors in individual counseling sessions, they would also be just as effective when used with groups of students. In addition to producing new behavior, they might be used to modify maladaptive behavior. The group environment itself could serve as an additional aid in accomplishing such a task. Since many of the problem behaviors brought to the attention of a counselor stem from inappropriate interactions with the social environment and since frequently the peer group is a prestigeful group for influencing adolescent behavior, it would seem logical to use both the social environment and the peer group to correct such behaviors. With any type of theoretically based counseling, group processes are more efficient with certain types of problems and inappropriate for others.

The use of learning principles in counseling, however, gives even greater credence to the group process. (1) There are greater numbers of varieties of models within a group; (2) there are greater numbers of sources of reinforcement within the group; (3) there are more opportunities for creating realistic social enactments whereby role rehearsal can be practiced, changed, and strengthened; (4) there is an immediate situation in which generalization as well as discrimination can be learned with greater efficiency; and (5) membership in the group itself can be utilized as a powerful reinforcing agency. The simulation of social reality and social environment created by a group can be systematically controlled and manipulated to bring about, in the group, the learning or change in behavior that each individual and the group collectively have agreed upon—this fact is of great significance for behavioral group counseling.

Research Related to Behavioral Group Counseling

The literature abounds with research done to study the relevant variables of groups and group dynamics. Some of these studies offer support for the validity of behavioral group counseling theory. A typical example is the study done by Asch (1952) in which he demonstrated that group opinion and observation of the expression of group and individual judgment can affect the immediate observable behavior of people. The majority of the subjects in his experiment actually denied their sensory judgment in expressing the relative length of lines following the exposure to confederates acting as models. They conformed to the judgment of others. However, for the present purposes of more interest are the recent studies that have been conducted to demonstrate behavioral counseling concepts in group situations. As Petrullo (1962) has indicated, much of the present and past research has not tried to develop techniques for bringing about cures, but rather it has been done to try to develop concepts which would enable researchers to understand behavior, or sometimes to predict it. Since results in terms of changed or developed behaviors are the important aspects of behavioral counseling, only those studies which have attempted to demonstrate these results are of significance for our present topic.

Johnson (1964) did a study with fourth- fifth-, and sixth-grade students for the purpose of testing a procedure for increasing classroom verbal participation. The subjects were children who had participated very little or none at all in their normal classroom situations. The experimental groups were formed on the basis of a teacher's ranking of students according to degree of participation in class. Each treatment group was composed of three children. In some treatment groups, all were low participators. Other treatment groups were made up of two low participators and one high participator. Still in others, there was placed a low and two high participators. Two control groups were used, one of which was removed from the classroom to view movies and another which remained in the classroom.

The experimental groups were taken from class and given five thirty-minute treatment sessions administered once every other school day for two weeks. The treatment consisted of discussions led by the counselor on topics that each pupil was likely to have opinions or knowledge of, such as a child's favorite TV program or what they liked to do after school. Whenever a low participator contributed to the discussion, the counselor gave positive verbal reinforcement but withheld such verbal reinforcement when a high participator made a contribution.

Three criterion measures were used: (1) the teacher's rating of verbal behavior during the weeks of the experiment; (2) the degree of participation in a controlled discussion led by a counselor who was a stranger to the students; and (3) observation of classroom verbal participation by an independent observer. (This observer recorded the frequency of verbal participation of each pupil within one week after completion of the treatment.)

The findings of the study indicated that the low participator students who received the reinforcement engaged in more verbal participation than the control groups on all three criterion tests. Such differences were only significant, however, on the teacher ratings and the observation of classroom verbal participation. This would suggest evidence that the experimental treatment did generalize to a situation outside the treatment group. In general, greater transfer to classroom participation occurred when the treatment groups consisted of all low participators rather than when one or two high participators were mixed with the group.

The Krumboltz and Thoresen (1964) study, reported earlier, also included reinforcement counseling in group settings, as well as model-reinforcement counseling with groups. The subjects for this study were eleventh-grade students who had volunteered for future educational and vocational counseling. The purpose of the study was to encourage students to take action that would provide them with accurate and realistic information relevant to their future plans. If a student asked a question or made a comment showing interest or deliberation regarding finding information, the counselor would encourage this by appropriate comments such as, "I'm glad you asked that question. . . ."; or "That sounds like a good thing to do."

In addition to such verbal reinforcement, the counselor also structured cues that would lead to the consideration of important questions, such as asking the question, "What would be some good ways to get the information that you want?"

At the end of each group session, the counselor asked each subject to summarize the specific steps which he might use to get information about his future plans. These summaries were again reinforced by the counselor who then may have added any specific steps that the student did not mention. Students were told to begin working on some of their suggestions; these actions could then be reviewed at the second counseling session which would take place approximately one week later.

For the students in the group and individual model-reinforcement counseling, an additional feature was added to what has been described. With these students, a fifteen-minute model interview with a high school boy who asked questions and suggested possible information sources was also used. In this way, students observed the model student being reinforced by the model counselor for the questions and information-seeking ideas he presented.

The criterion consisted of the frequency and variety of student information-seeking which occurred outside of the counseling sessions during a three-week period of time following the first counseling interview. Subjects were interviewed by other members of the research team, not their counselors, so that the interviewers were not aware of the treatment students had received.

Students were asked to describe any information-seeking about educational or career opportunities they had performed during the three-week interval, and a random sample of the subjects' reports was validated for accuracy.

Whereas the results indicated that the reinforcement and model-reinforcement methods produced more criterion behavior than did the equivalent control groups, no significant difference between the group and individual counseling settings was indicated. Due to the significant interaction between the schools where the study was conducted, attention was directed to differing preferences among the treatment counselors for group and individual counseling. In four of the six schools, students who had group counseling engaged in slightly more information-seeking than the subjects who had received individual counseling. The reverse was true for the other two schools. It is quite likely that these differences may reflect the preference of a counselor for a particular method of counseling as well as their own effectiveness with groups as opposed to individuals.

Ryan (1966) did a study to test effectiveness of model-reinforcement group counseling, using naïve student-counselors, to improve study habits of college students. In addition to examining the effectiveness of a technique, she was interested in investigating critical variables of models with respect to effectiveness in administering reinforcement. The uniqueness of the study is due to the fact that she used live-model counselors rather than audio- or video-models as in previous studies reported.

The criterion was defined as favorable study behavior, as measured by the Study Habits Inventory. Student model-counselors were designated as high-, medium-, or low-model counselors based on their GPA and head resident recommendation. These models performed by providing cues and appropriate reinforcement to favorable study habit responses on the part of the college students in the groups. An active and inactive control group was established for comparative purposes.

Ryan's results supported the effectiveness of model-reinforcement group counseling on increase of students' effective study behavior and gave some evidence supporting a rationale for using non-professionals as high-model student-counselors. Although the differences between the categories of models did not reach significance, the trend was to obtain higher scores for treatment in groups where the high-model counselor was present. The data clearly indicated that the most effective means for increasing students use of effective study behavior was the combination of reinforcement counseling with the high-model student-counselor. This study is particularly significant for school group counselors who may systematically utilize student members of a group for reinforcement or modeling activities.

Beach (1967) did a study with seventh- and eighth-grade underachieving students using group counseling models. Subjects for the experiment did not volunteer for counseling, but were identified and assigned to groups for counseling. One experimental group listened to a taped model of a group of underachieving students. On the tapes, students were reinforced for achievement-oriented statements regarding future behavior. Her results indicate that the group model-reinforcement treatment was significantly more effective than control group situations where boys were the subjects. She did not find that the use of such tapes was significantly effective with girls. The criterion measure was improved GPA. Beach did, however, find significant individual differences among students, with respect to exposure to the group model tapes. Her findings suggest the importance of investigating personality differences correlated with degree of responsiveness to social imitation.

A series of studies have recently been completed on systematic desensitization in groups for the purpose of reducing examination anxiety (Laemmle and Thoresen, 1968; Neuman, 1968; Weinstein, 1968). For the Weinstein study, criteria measured were (1) self-report on the Thayer Activation Adjective Check List, (2) responses on the Test Anxiety Inventory, and (3) responses on the Test Anxiety Rating Scale. In addition to these criteria, Neuman measured the heart rate of students immediately preceding an actual exam and obtained trained observer ratings of motor response during the exam. Laemmle and Thoresen used telemetry equipment to measure the heart rate of students before, during, and after the taking of an exam. Telemetry equipment, which is a type of transistor device, permits continuous monitoring of heart rates of subjects in natural settings, such as during the taking of exams. All these studies indicated that test anxiety could be reduced or modified through the process of desensitization as evaluated on the criterion measures.

Paul and Shannon (1966) did a careful study of intense interpersonal anxiety in a public speaking situation using four types of groups, two control procedures, and several criteria. Among these were self-report, GPA, and anxiety test scores. The experimental design was so constructed that knowledge could be obtained regarding the differential effectiveness of individual versus small group desensitization, generalized attention-placebo, and insight-oriented treatments. Significant results were obtained in nine group sessions. Additional information was gained regarding the roles of group counselors and specific data about what actually occurred in the group sessions.

It is becoming increasingly apparent that the training of counselors to administer reinforcement is a critical factor in its effectiveness. In addition, greater refinement in assessing relevant reinforcement for *what* groups of students, in *what* situations, regarding *what* problems is required if this technique is to be more powerful. Likewise, further investigation is necessary regarding the characteristics and qualifications of models used in behavioral counseling. (Many of the studies cited have shown differential effects for boys and girls receiving counseling related to the sex of the models and the subjects.)

Some of these issues were noted in the studies done by Thoresen and Stewart (1967, 1968). Again model-reinforcement techniques were used with groups. In some treatments, the counselor *systematically* reinforced students on criterion statements. In other treatments, the counselor *randomly* reinforced statements. Although the reinforcement counseling produced more significant results than the control procedure, no significant difference was found between the systematic reinforcement and the random reinforcement procedures.

Analysis of the tape recordings of group sessions showed that counselors in the systematic reinforcement treatment failed to differentially reinforce criterion statements. Consequently, both treatments consisted, to a degree, of random reinforcement. This points to the need of careful and thorough training of counselors using this technique.

For further details and more comprehensive descriptions of such studies and additional examples of the application of behavioral techniques in counseling, the reader is referred to Krumboltz and Thoresen (Eds.), *Behavioral Counseling: Cases and Techniques*, Holt, Rinehart and Winston (in press).

UNIQUE ASPECTS OF BEHAVIORAL GROUP COUNSELING

Certain features of this approach to group counseling stand out as unique when compared with traditional group processes. These qualities of uniqueness may even be distasteful to some counselors who have a bias for interpretive counseling. They are, however, critical to the behavioral approach. These areas are the following:

1. The goals for group counseling are distinctly specified and agreed upon *in advance* by each member individually and the group collectively.
2. The goals are specified according to behavioral terminology so that the outcome of the goal may be observed and evaluated at the conclusion of the group sessions.

3. Only one unit of behavior is dealt with at one time. Successive behaviors may be considered in turn which may lead to the performing of more complex units of behavior.
4. A systematic plan for achieving the goal is developed by the counselor, *before* the group counseling begins, involving a choice of techniques that will be used for counseling.
5. Both verbal and nonverbal techniques may be used.
6. The counselor takes an active and important role in the process, frequently taking the lead in directing the discussions.

Further elaboration of these points may provide clarification of their uniqueness.

Goals Are Specific and Predetermined

From personal experience with traditional group counseling, the author is aware of the ambiguity with which many groups have begun. It is obvious to students beginning a group that there is a lack of clarity about its purpose based on the fact that they ask what they are to do or what the group is supposed to accomplish. In establishing these groups, the author took careful pains to interview each student regarding his desire to be a member of the group and would usually say something like, "I've noticed that you seem confused about what you want out of school, where you are going in the future, or perhaps life in general. I'm wondering if you would like to join a group of students who have indicated they are equally confused. We would meet on a regular basis to discuss these problems." Usually the student's face would brighten and he would agree to join. Consequently, a group was formed based on confusion, not the least of which was that of the counselor's who was not sure where the group was to go from this dismal beginning.

This should not be the case in behavioral group work. The private interview is equally, if not more, important to the process. Here, the counselor attempts to assess, through discussion with the student, what is causing the confusion. Is it that the student does not know what is expected of him at school? Does he not know where to get relevant information regarding alternatives of the future? Does he not know how to evaluate the relative importance of these alternatives in his value system? Is he confused about his role in society—how people react to what he does—or confused regarding how to perform the role he feels is expected of him? All of these questions might be applicable to this student. Each question should be dealt with singularly and each should be considered according to its relative importance *to the student.* If the student decides that not knowing how to act in certain social situations is the source of greatest confusion, then this is *his* goal and he has agreed that this is something he would like to work on.

When the counselor has talked to other students who have this similar goal, then a group can be constituted to accomplish that purpose. Each one knows what he wants from the group and recognizes that together they will work towards helping the others and themselves to achieve this.

This type of specification of group goals may lead to the formation of groups not usually considered for group counseling. In the studies cited, groups were engaged in exploratory behavior associated with education and vocational decisions. In the Johnson study, children were to increase the frequency with which they spoke in class; in the Paul and Shannon study, the group was constituted to reduce anxiety in giving public speeches. It is conceivable that groups might be established for the purpose of girls learning to be comfortable in the presence of boys; students learning how to discuss a point of difference with teachers; or students specifically working on learning to show appreciation to other people. These usually are not considered counseling problems that merit time and effort in groups, yet these are problems that may lead to maladaptive behavior. Such groups would mean that counselors may be working with students they would not see in counseling in any other way. It is obvious why this might seem desirable to both the students and the counselors.

Goals Defined in Behavioral Terms

Lack of knowledge or indefiniteness can be hidden behind global or abstract words that mean different things to individuals.

"Self-concept" is a frequently used counseling term. Yet when a counselor is asked to say what things a person does differently when he has an improved "self-concept," the counselor may find this hard to do. By using global or abstract terms, such as "aggression," "frustration," "self-realization," the burden of definition of what is meant is placed on the reader or listener. Used in counseling, no clear-cut direction is given as to what is going on in the counseling process. Consequently, behavioral counselors define goals in terms of behaviors. If "aggressive" behavior is to be modified, the question is asked, "What type of aggressive behavior does this child exhibit and in what situations?" The answer may be that the goal is to stop Kevin from hitting other children on the playground during recess. Examples of behavioral group goals stated in these terms would be to increase the frequency of participation in class discussions; and to increase the ability of asking a teacher about a grade on a paper. Such definitions assist the counselor in selecting the techniques that will be used to achieve the goal.

Behavior Is Dealt With in Single Units

If a variety of problems are attacked simultaneously, it is unlikely that any of them will be solved efficiently, or even adequately; whereas, it is quite likely that solving one problem may cause an individual to be able to solve some related problems on his own. It is quite true that many problems are interrelated, which only means that correcting one may lead to assistance on the others. This does not mean that when the opportunity arises within a group situation to attend to a related problem, it is ignored. During a recent group session with seventh-grade students working on the task of learning to plan their time more effectively, the author had such an opportunity. Whenever Jeff would make a comment, he would literally shout his comment, drowning out anyone else who might be speaking at the time. Although this was extremely annoying to the counselor, she refrained from saying anything, hoping that one of the students would bring it up.

Finally Brad said, "Keep your voice down, Jeff." The counselor picked up the cue and said, "I wonder why you feel you have to shout, Jeff?" A girl remarked that Jeff did it to get attention. Jeff responded by saying that since he had so many brothers and sisters, he had to shout to be heard at home. One student then bet that Jeff couldn't be silent for five minutes, a challenge which Jeff accepted. This gave him time to cool down and be removed from the immediate center of attention. Following the five minutes, Jeff indicated he had a comment, and it was acknowledged. As he spoke, his voice was low and well-modulated and was immediately reinforced by the group with smiles and nods. The counselor also immediately reinforced this speaking behavior by complimenting him not only on his comment, but on the manner and volume level in which it was given. Subsequent comments from Jeff throughout the session and the following one were given more quietly and only made when Jeff had the floor and when no one else was speaking. This, too, was reinforced.

A Systematic Plan, Including Techniques, Is Predetermined

After the goal has been defined and before the first group meeting, the counselor decides on what techniques to use and in what sequence. For example, in dealing with social embarrassment in the presence of boys, a counselor may decide to begin with a prepared model of a girl discussing the problem with a counselor. In such an interview, the girl would suggest possible things she could do to feel more relaxed and to learn to be natural with a boy. Following the showing of such a model to the group, the counselor may have a group discussion based on the model in which the counselor would systematically reinforce any suggestions that the girls in the group might make. Then she might decide to use a model of a girl actually engaged in a social interaction with a boy, and this would be followed by discussion. Still later, she might use roleplaying where girls practice talking with a boy, each girl being reinforced by the counselor and by her peers for those things she did well. Finally, the counselor might have the girls practice in real situations, beginning with talking to their fathers or brothers, and reporting back to the group. Eventually, the girls would practice on some boys in a class or other related school activity.

Throughout all of this, the counselor should have decided what types of statements and behavior were to be reinforced and what method of reinforcement would be used. Keeping a chart to record attempts made in appropriate situations might be a method of reinforcement, as well as the approval given by the counselor and group members. Eventually, the success the girl experiences in trying this out in natural situations would come to be the maintaining reinforcement.

Methods and Activities May Be Varied

From the previous example used, it is apparent that various methods may be used in this type of counseling. In addition to reinforcement, verbal or physical modeling (prepared, or real-life) and role rehearsal, other methods may be devised. The use of a simulated person in the Life Career Game used in group counseling (Varenhorst, 1968) is an innovative technique for group work. The Game is a particularly powerful tool for group counseling related to problems of decision-making, vocational and educational planning, as well as social interactions and problem-solving. A unique aspect of this technique is that it provides a simulated person that can be manipulated by students in the group. Consequently, they can try out activities they desire for themselves without having to reveal these desires openly. Many types of learning might be provided through simulation techniques.

The Counselor Takes an Active Role

Not only the development of a systematic plan, but its implementation rests with the counselor. This necessitates that the counselor assume a more active role in this type of group process as opposed to the usual situation in traditional groups. Likewise, a counselor himself frequently serves as a model for the particular behavior to be learned which would also account for a more active counselor role in the group.

Finally, since goals have been defined before the group begins, a definite termination point is provided. This is not always true in traditional groups. It is stressed here that the evaluation of the success of achieving the goal is the extent to which this behavior generalizes to situations outside the counseling setting. Since the goals are behavioral, their success can be observed and determined.

SPECIAL CONSIDERATIONS FOR BEHAVIORAL COUNSELING

The Counselor

Frequent use has been made, throughout this chapter, of the word "systematic." This has been applied to the control of environment, the presentation of reinforcement, and the development of a plan, to mention a few such references. It is quite obvious that human beings do not tend to be systematic, particularly when it comes to behavior. This fact places a heavy burden on the behavioral group counselor. It has been suggested in the studies that have been cited that inconclusive results may have been due to the *un*systematic application of the treatment on the part of a counselor. This is probably due to differing biases regarding the process itself. It may also be due to the fact that counselors are subject to the same principles of behavior control that they are attempting to use. Counselors respond to reinforcement given by students, and their behavior is controlled by what happens in their environment. The example of Johnny is a good illustration of how a student may control the adult world of the school. In order to systematically control a counseling environment, a counselor must be aware of his susceptibility to these factors and consciously control them in order to be effective. This is a most difficult feat to accomplish.

Historically, in the field of psychotherapy, the need for personal therapy has been stressed. The rationale for this is that a therapist needs to know himself and his customary ways of dealing with problems before he can help others. The same holds true for behavioral counselors. Thorough knowledge of the effect of environmental stimuli on his own behavior is required by the counselor. Only when he knows his own system of rewards, responsiveness to imitation, inflexibility in adapting to situations, etc., can he adequately be in control of the environment of others. Recognizing the variables which maintain the behavior in his own life will aid him in helping others to modify their behavior.

To allow for this, careful training in the principles and use of the method is a necessity. At Stanford University, the theory itself has been used to train the counselors who will use it. Such training should extend beyond the use of techniques to training in assessment in recognizing *behaviors* and in thinking in terms of *behaviors* of people rather than traits or abstractions.

The matter of assessment is critical in behavioral counseling. Many students and clients are not able to identify the behavior they want modified nor do they recognize their reward system. This means that the counselor must know how to identify or evaluate such information from the present behavior of the student. Assessment must include the defining of the problem to be modified, the identification of the factors that are maintaining the present behavior, the sources of reward for *this* individual, the resources available to the counselor to deal with the problem and whether or not the problem is one of deficiency in the behavior repertoire, or a behavior that has been inhibited, i.e., is it a learning problem or a performance problem? Not all of this information may be immediately or readily available. Therefore, a counselor will have to be skilled in ways of obtaining information through questioning and observations. This type of assessment is directed primarily to the *present* situation rather than to past history of child rearing and experience. What the counselor wants to know is what is supporting the behavior at the present time, and what is available currently to help change the behavior.

Finally, contrary to what is frequently believed, a very critical aspect of successful behavioral counseling is the relationship which is established between the counselor and his group, or his client. Unless a relationship of warmth, respect, and high prestige exists in such a relationship, any reinforcement given by the counselor, or modeling done by the counselor, will be greatly reduced in effectiveness or be nonexistent. However, again contrary to what has been professed, the counselor needs skill in developing a variety of relationships with his client or group. Although the counseling profession has traditionally clung to the need for a warm, accepting relationship with students, at times, in behavior counseling, such warmth and acceptance may not be conducive to the process of change. As Thoresen (1968) has suggested, in the complex social-psychological phenomenon where the behavior of counselor and student is being influenced, a variety of counselor-student "relationships" may be demanded. A counselor, in his role, must be able to draw upon a different kind of relationship with different students in the same group at the same time, and different kinds of relationships with the same student at different times. A flexibility on the part of the counselor mutually influences what is identified as an appropriate or "good" relationship. Again, what results from the establishing of different modes of relating is the criterion against which to evaluate the "goodness" or "badness" of a relationship.

Associated with this concept is the fact that the counselor must mobilize a group to work together towards its common goal. As Krumboltz (1968) has said, "Somehow the accomplishment of each individual's goal must become the united goal of the entire group. Only then can the full force and effectiveness of the group be brought to bear on each individual's problem. Only then will each individual be maximally influenced by the group" (p. 4). This is the responsibility of the group counselor in molding the group that will work to help each member accomplish the member's own goal.

The Student's Role

It has been mentioned previously that the peer group itself can be used to influence the behavior of individual members within the group. In behavioral terms, students can be trained to give appropriate reinforcement and to serve as models for the group. With a group goal clearly defined and with each member committed to this goal, students can be trained to help one another reach the goal. There is no hidden agenda, nor hidden dynamic, that the counselor attempts to implement throughout the group sessions. What is being done is open and direct, which seems far more efficient and self-correcting than traditional group practices.

An example of this would be an extension of the Ryan study using naive college students who were trained to give cues and administer verbal reinforcement to study-oriented statements for members of the group. Students can be cued to show approval to other members who demonstrate or respond with desirable behaviors. As this develops, the corporate group's expectations and approval can be a powerful agent for change.

The Life Career Game (Varenhorst, 1968), as previously cited, is an excellent example of how this works. During the game, students work in teams of two planning the life of the hypothetical student. In group discussions that follow each round of the game, students reveal what plans and decisions they have made for their person. Since all teams are working with the same person, each team serves as a model of a decision-maker and the effectiveness or validity of these decisions are mutually discussed by all members of the group. This simulates life as it exists in reality, with the added benefit of students learning from their simulated person's experiences *before* they are required to make such decisions with respect to their own lives.

Composition of the Group: Membership

Many of the guidelines used for constituting groups have been borrowed from what has been learned from fairly extensive research in the field of group dynamics. Thoresen (1967) views this as a promising change as increased efforts are being made to correlate the two almost independent fields: group counseling and group dynamics. Such knowledge is being applied to both traditional and behavioral group work.

Schachter, Ellertson, McBride, and Gregory (1960) demonstrated that the more attractive the group may appear to a member of the group, the more likely he will work for the cohesiveness of the group. Some subjects were told either that there was every reason to expect that the other members of the group would like them and they would like members of the groups, or were told that it had not been possible to bring a congenial group together so there was no particular reason to think they would like the group or that the group would like them. Subjects who were led to expect they would like and be liked did in fact like the group members significantly more than those who were led to expect the opposite.

Even the manipulation of expectations regarding similarity of opinion between a group and a member can influence the attractiveness of a group. Festinger, Schachter, and Back (1950) demonstrated this by telling group members that the group either held similar or dissimilar opinions to their own. Even though the groups were formed at random, the members who were led to expect that the group held similar opinions to their own liked the group more than did those members who were led to expect that divergent opinions existed in the group.

Aronson and Mills (1960) found that when students go through a great deal of trouble or pain to attain membership in a group, they tend to value it more highly than a person who attains such membership with a minimum of effort. This, perhaps, is the rationale for the severe initiation practices of "prestigeful" clubs or organizations.

Although these factors must be considered in behavior group composition, other factors may be just as pertinent. The main criterion should be the commonality of the problem to be considered. As has been previously stressed, the delineation of this common problem needs to be more specific than it might be in traditional groups. Consideration also must be given to the inclusion of appropriate members who might contribute to the achievement of the goal. This may mean that the question of homogeneous versus heterogeneous groups becomes a question of homogenity of goals and heterogenity of age group, personalities, intelligence, or sex.

Personality traits, age, and sex do seem to be critical factors. Although studies, for the most part, are inconclusive, some evidence has been gathered regarding the responsiveness to conditioning and imitation as they are associated with these factors. In his chapter on responsiveness to social stimuli, Patterson (1965) discusses his investigations on early training practices and their effect on subsequent responsiveness to social stimuli. He found this variable of responsiveness to social stimuli as having at least three components: responsiveness to social approval and disapproval, imitation, and ability to discriminate among social cues. He finds support for the notion that the parent and the peer culture are conditioned to place particular value on certain classes of behaviors in the child. He demonstrated that children adopt highly stable sequences or patterns of responses, which make it impossible to change a child's behavior by the schedules of reinforcement that were used in his study. He summarizes part of his findings as, "The variables that relate significantly to the responsiveness of the child to positive social reinforcement are: age of the child, the status of the peer, and the interaction between sex of parent and sex of child" (p. 168). Also, "Permissive parental practices are associated with greater responsiveness to social reinforcers delivered by the same-sexed parent. Restrictive parental practices are associated with greater responsiveness to social approval of the opposite-sexed parent and to social disapproval dispensed by either parent" (p. 175). Although these factors are not always easy to assess, perhaps they should be given consideration in deciding on the composition of a group.

Behavioral group counseling has been used with some degree of success with various aged groups: (Johnson, 1964), elementary aged children; (Krumboltz and Thoresen, 1964), secondary school students; and (Ryan, 1966), college-level students. One of the questions raised by Beach (1967) was whether or not seventh- or eighth-grade students were too young to be sufficiently responsive to the type of model-reinforcement counseling that was used in her study. Further research is needed to answer this question.

The sex factor has been investigated in a number of studies (Beach, 1967; Hosford, 1966; Krumboltz and Thoresen, 1964; Varenhorst, 1964). Some of these studies were related to the effect of models on females as opposed to males; others studied the interaction between the sex of the model and the sex of the group. It is possible that in some areas it would be important for the sex of the model to be the same as the sex of a group, and for other areas, it would be important to have a heterosexual-homogeneous group using both male and female models. It has been found in the author's experience with the use of the Life Career Game in group counseling that it is an advantage to have both sexes in the groups and that heterogeneity of ages and abilities was desirable in constituting the groups.

Composition of the Group: Size

The same issues regarding size associated with traditional groups are applicable to behavioral groups. As Krumboltz

(1968) has indicated, no experimental evidence is available on optimal group size in behavioral counseling. Goldstein, Heller, and Sechrest (1966) have summarized some of the outcome effects associated with group size that have been investigated, primarily in the field of group dynamics. In general, they found that as the size of groups is increased, the group leader talks more, the average member talks less, the proportion of very infrequent contributors increases, more members report feelings of threat and inhibition regarding participation, the rate of giving information and suggestions increases while the rate of asking for opinions and showing agreement decreases, there is more dependency on the leader, sense of belonging decreases, feelings of frustration increase, cohesiveness decreases, and subgroups and cliques increase. Some of these effects would be of advantage while working on some types of problems in behavioral counseling.

However, for some behavior modification, it is more efficient to use groups the size of an average class, assembly-hall-size groups, or even mass audiences. In the author's experience with groups using the Career Game, she found that considerably less discussion took place in groups of fifty, whereas a class of thirty students worked successfully and more effectively than a group of eight. With this technique, the more examples of decision-making that arise from greater numbers is an advantage. However, it was found that when students were of low ability, it was only effective in groups of no more than six. These students require much more individual attention and more encouragement in expressing their thoughts.

LIMITATIONS OF BEHAVIORAL GROUP COUNSELING

The chief limitation of this process is that it is not as simple as it sounds. Contributing to this is the need for many more research studies to investigate variables necessary to the process. More research will have to be done with many more varieties of problems, studying characteristics of counselors, types of reinforcement, and varieties of models, just to mention a few such types. Although mention has been made or implied throughout the chapter of limiting factors, a brief elaboration may be helpful.

1. Rewards and reinforcement: It was stated earlier that the frequency of emitted behavior is the prime operational definition of reinforcing stimuli. This means that the only evidence that an object or a response is a reinforcer is whether it affects the frequency of behavior which it follows. It has been assumed that certain comments, such as "good," "hmm-hum," and "fine" are reinforcing and that candy, money, and recognition will reinforce behavior. This may be true for some individuals, but perhaps not true for others. It has been found that using "good" and "fine" affects the behavior of low socio-economic children, but not middle class children. For middle class students, the words "right" or "correct" are reinforcing (Krasner and Ullmann, 1965, p. 158-159). Thoresen and Stewart (1967, 1968) found that statements usually considered reinforcing did not significantly affect subsequent behavior whether they were applied systematically or randomly. Perhaps such statements were not rewarding to the students involved.

Such evidence points to the need to obtain more accurate information as to what is reinforcing with which students. This may mean that counselors will have to study the environments of students to assess what they react to, their present patterns of behavior, their interests, fads, and values. Such assessments may have to extend into their homes and their extra-curricular activities, much in the manner of Patterson's work. Unraveling the intricate web of stimuli maintaining and affecting behavior is a complex task.

2. Use of models: The same problems are related to the choice of models for counseling. Although social psychologists have accumulated much information regarding characteristics of models, relatively few of these have been researched in counseling environments. Three studies have been done to investigate the interaction between student characteristics and model characteristics in such a setting, and they represent a fruitful start to future research.

Thoresen and Krumblotz (in press) have reported on the first of these studies. They explored the relationship between the athletic success of a high school male model presented on an audio-tape and self-ratings of athletic success of male clients.

Three levels of models were used: high, medium, and low. They found that the high athletic success model was most effective for all students who observed the models. As a second part of this study, the same authors looked at differentiated academic success models and their effect on students. The differences in high, medium, and low models were created by biographic introductions to the models, including items such as membership in California Scholarship Federation, GPA, and other academic activities. Again the subjects of the experiment gave self-ratings of themselves as students. In this study, no significant differences were found. However, the students who rated themselves as high academic success students did engage in more academic tasks than did the other students. Hosford (1966) did the second study in this series, and Thoresen, Hosford, and Krumboltz (1968) did a third study examining the characteristics of models in terms of academic, athletic, and social success. All of these studies point to the question of appropriate ways of presenting model characteristics, as well as relevant criterion measures.

3. Systematic control of environment: When dealing with any human being, it is always hard to predict his behavior. However, it is far easier to systematically apply behavioral techniques in individual counseling than it is in group counseling. The more individuals added to a group, the more complex become the variables affecting the group. Consequently, systematically controlling the environmental stimuli produced by a variety of individuals makes group work in behavioral terms quite difficult. It can be said again, more knowledge is needed regarding human behavior before behavioral group counseling becomes a less complicated process.

Conclusion

At a time when greater demands are being made to demonstrate the viability of counseling and group counseling in particular, behavioral group counseling merits serious attention. Despite its limitations and complexities, support can be given for its efficiency and success. For one, the author, who has done both traditional and behavioral counseling, prefers the behavioral method. Such preference is based not only on the comforting sense of order and specificity which it provides for the counselor who uses it, but also on the evidence that it is assisting students to develop adaptive behaviors. Further, competence at one level is being seen translated or generalized to other levels of a client's life. This would seem to be the function of counseling. At long last, some counselors who use this method are being rewarded by seeing the evidence of their work. If this be so, then according to behavioral learning principles, we should see an increase in the number of counselors who begin applying this therapy to their counseling.

SUMMARY

Principles of learning which define the manner in which behavior is acquired and modified have been applied to the counseling process. Such principles as operant conditioning through reinforcement, extinction, and modeling form the basis for behavioral group counseling.

The uniqueness of this theory of counseling is that it leads to the creation and use of a variety of techniques and methods to achieve the purpose of counseling, i.e., to change behavior.

Behavioral group counseling differs from other theories of group work in several ways: (1) The goals for counseling are distinctly specified *before* counseling begins. (2) These goals are stated in behavioral terms rather than in global or abstract terms. (3) Single units of behavior are concentrated on at one time. (4) A variety of activities may take place within the group, including both verbal and nonverbal techniques. (5) The counselor is more active in the group. (6) Behavioral results which do or do not generalize to situations outside the counseling setting can be evaluated. Such evaluation may lead to a self-correcting process. (7) Completion of the goal provides a defined termination point.

Kurt Lewin (1947) observed, following several of his studies, that the behavior of individuals is usually easier to change when they are formed into a group than to change any one of them separately. This has been supported to a degree by the experimental work done on behavioral group counseling. It has been found that the variety of sources for reinforcement and modeling contained within a group offers a rich field for behavior modification. The prestige of group membership itself can be utilized as a reinforcing stimulus.

The effective group counselor must have skill in systematically using group dynamics for the group's purposes, be trained in assessment which is focused on the present situation rather than the past, and be flexible in establishing differing relationships with students as the situation demands.

The behavioral group process is limited by the lack of information regarding specifics of variables governing human behavior. There are no universal, consistent reinforcements, and people differ regarding their responsiveness to conditioning, including imitation. As more knowledge is gathered about such factors, and as counselors are better trained, the field of guidance will see greater use of this type of counseling.

REFERENCES

Aronson, E., and Mills, J.: The affect of severity of initiation on liking for a group. In D. Cartwright and A. Zander (Eds.): *Group Dynamics.* Evanston, Ill.: Row, Peterson, 1960. pp. 95-104.

Asch, S. E.: *Social Psychology.* New York: Prentice-Hall, 1952.

Beach, A. I.: The effect of group model-reinforcement counseling on achievement behavior of seventh and eighth grade students. Unpublished doctoral dissertation, Stanford University, 1967.

Bruner, F.: The effect of programmed instruction on information-seeking behavior in tenth grade students. Unpublished doctoral dissertation, Stanford University, 1965.

Dollard, J., and Miller, N. E.: *Personality and Psychotherapy.* New York: McGraw-Hill, 1950.

Festinger, L.; Schachter, S., and Back, K.: *Social Pressures in Informal Groups.* New York: Harper, 1950.

Goldstein, A. P.; Heller, K., and Sechrest, L. B.: *Psychotherapy and the Psychology of Behavior Change.* New York: Wiley, 1966.

Greenspoon, J.: Verbal conditioning and clinical psychology. In A. J. Bachrach (Ed.): *Experimental Foundations of Clinical Psychology.* New York: Basic Books, 1962. pp. 510-554.

Hilgard, E. R.: *Introduction to Psychology.* (3rd ed.) New York: Harcourt, 1962.

Hosford, R. E.: Determining effective models for counseling clients of varying competencies. Unpublished doctoral dissertation, Stanford University, 1966.

Hull, C. L.: *Principles of Behavior.* New York: Appleton-Century-Crofts, 1943.

Johnson, C. J.: Reinforcing verbal participation in treatment groups of varying composition. Unpublished doctoral dissertation, Stanford University, 1964.

Krasner, L.: The use of generalized reinforcers in psychotherapy research. *Psychological Reports,* 1955, *1,* 19-25.

Krasner, L., and Ullmann, L. P.: *Research in Behavior Modification.* New York: Holt, Rinehart and Winston, 1965.

Krumboltz, J. D.: Promoting adaptive behavior: New answers to familiar questions. In J. D. Krumboltz (Ed.): *Revolution in Counseling.* New York: Houghton-Mifflin, 1966. pp. 3-27.

Krumboltz, J. D.: A behavioral approach to group counseling and therapy. *Journal of Research and Development in Education,* 1968, *1,* 3-19.

Krumboltz, J. D., and Thoresen, C. E.: The effects of behavioral counseling in group and individual settings on information-seeking behavior. *Journal of Counseling Psychology,* 1964, *11,* 324-333.

Krumboltz, J. D., and Schroeder, W. W.: Promoting career exploration through reinforcement. *Personnel and Guidance Journal,* 1965, *44,* 19-26.

Krumboltz, J. D.: Varenhorst, B. B., and Thoresen, C. E.: Non-verbal factors in the effectiveness of models in counseling. *Journal of Counseling Psychology,* 1967, *14,* 412-418.

Krumboltz, J. D., and Thoresen, C. E. (Eds.): *Behavioral Counseling: Cases and Techniques.* New York: Holt, Rinehart and Winston, (in press).

Laemmle, P. E., and Thoresen, C. E.: Physiological measures as outcome criteria in group desensitization. Paper presented at the American Educational Research Association Convention, Chicago, February 1968.

Lazarus, A. A.: The results of behavior therapy in 126 cases of severe neurosis. *Behavior Research Therapy,* 1963, *136,* 272-278.

Lewin, K.: Group decision and social change. In T. M. Newcomb and E. L. Hartley (Eds.): *Readings in Social Psychology.* New York: Henry Holt, 1947. pp. 330-344.

Neuman, D.: The effect of imagery arousal level in group desensitization. Paper presented at the American Educational Research Association Convention, Chicago, February 1968.

Patterson, G. R.: Responsiveness to social stimuli. In L. Krasner and L. P. Ullmann (Eds.): *Research in Behavior Modification.* New York: Holt, Rinehart and Winston, 1965. pp. 157-179.

Paul, G. L., and Shannon, D. T.: Treatment of anxiety through systematic desensitization in therapy groups. *Journal of Abnormal Psychology,* 1966, *71,* 124-135.

Pavlov, I. P.: *Conditioned Reflexes.* London: Oxford University Press, 1927.

Petrullo, L.: Small group research. In A. J. Bachrach (Ed.): *Experimental*

Foundations of Clinical Psychology. New York: Basic Books, 1962. pp. 211-253.

Ryan, T.: Model-reinforcement group counseling to modify study behavior. Paper read at American Personnel and Guidance Association Convention, Washington, D. C., April 1966.

Ryan, T., and Krumboltz, J. D.: Effect of planned reinforcement counseling on client decision-making behavior. *Journal of Counseling Psychology,* 1964, *11,* 315-323.

Schachter, S.; Ellertson, N.; McBride, D., and Gregory, D.: An experimental study of cohesiveness and productivity. In D. Cartwright and A. Zander (Eds.): *Group Dynamics.* Evanston, Illinois: Row, Peterson, 1960. pp. 152-162.

Skinner, B. F.: *Science and Human Behavior.* New York: Macmillan, 1953.

Thoresen, C. E.: Counseling in groups: "Not proven" but promising. Invited address for Lansing Area Personnel and Guidance Association, Lansing, Michigan, January 1967.

Thoresen, C. E.: Counselor as an applied behavioral scientist. Invited Address, Third Annual Research in Guidance Institute, University of Wisconsin, Madison, Wisconsin, June 1968.

Thoresen, C. E.; Krumboltz, J. D., and Varenhorst, B. B.: Sex of counselors and models: Effect on client career exploration. *Journal of Counseling Psychology,* 1967, *14,* 503-509.

Thoresen, C. E., and Stewart, N. R.: Counseling in groups: Using group social models. Paper presented at the American Educational Research Association Convention, New York, February 1967.

Thoresen, C. E.; Hosford, R. E., and Krumboltz, J. D.: Determining effective models for counseling clients of varying competencies. Unpublished manuscript, Stanford University, 1968.

Thoresen, C. E., and Stewart, N. R.: Developing and using social models and stimulus materials. Paper presented at the American Personnel and Guidance Association Convention, Detroit, April 1968.

Thoresen, C. E., and Krumboltz, J. D.: Similarity of social models and clients in behavioral counseling. Two experimental studies. *Journal of Counseling Psychology* (in press).

Ullmann, L. P., and Krasner, L. (Eds.): *Case Studies in Behavior Modification.* New York: Holt, Rinehart and Winston, 1965.

Varenhorst, B. B.: An experimental comparison of nonverbal factors in determining the effectiveness of models in counseling. Unpublished doctoral dissertation, Stanford University, 1964.

Varenhorst, B. B.: Innovative tool for group counseling: The Life Career Game. *School Counselor,* 1968, *15,* 357-363.

Weinstein, F.: The influence of psychological types on group desensitization. Paper presented at the American Educational Research Association Convention, Chicago, February, 1968.

Wolpe, J.: *Psychotherapy by Reciprocal Inhibition.* Stanford, California: Stanford University Press, 1958.

Wolpe, J.: The systematic desensitization treatment of neuroses. *Journal of Nervous and Mental Disease,* 1961, *132,* 189-203.

Wolpe, J.: The experimental foundations of some new psychotherapeutic methods. In A. J. Bachrach (Ed.): *Experimental Foundations of Clinical Psychology.* New York: Basic Books, 1962. pp. 554-575.

VI

GROUP COUNSELING AND
DEVELOPMENTAL PROCESSES

Warren C. Bonney

Interest in the functioning of small groups has become one of the most significant social phenomenon in post-World War II America. This interest has intensified and broadened even more greatly in the past ten years. *The trend appears to stem from the rapidly accelerating complexity with consequent need for group management of our social structure.* Large organizational and institutional efforts are dependent on basic small group factions for leadership and direction. *The small enduring group appears to be the basic functional element in modern society.* In order for these groups to function well, *cooperative effort is essential, which in turn demands some degree of indentification of the members with the group.*

The danger or threat of the trends described above to a progressing democratic society appears obvious. *If one cannot express and act on an individually evolved idea or belief without first insuring correspondence to the norms of his groups, his creative productions, and to a lesser degree, his creative potential, would be severely limited and eventually eliminated.* The trend of increased social complexity and urbanization may also affect the individual at a deeper and more significant level. For many an individual in our culture, his sense of self-identity, or "who am I," relies almost solely on his various group identifications. It would be difficult for many people to survive psychologically without these external definitions of self.

To rebel against or stand aloof from the trend towards social and individual control through group decisions may be individually noble but socially unproductive, if not destructive. The

157

inescapable but difficult solution is the fostering of a sense of individuality, initiative, and creativity within the group setting. The choice of slavish adherence to group norms or rebellion against them is, like most other dichotomous choices, unnecessary. Why cannot people be helped to realize their greatest creative potential within cooperative, cohesive groups? From experiences with counseling and psychotherapy groups, ad hoc laboratory groups, rifle squads, planning committees, and research teams, many of us have *come to believe that the most profound expression of individuality can be achieved through membership in a creative interdependent group.*

Much of the aim of group approaches such as counseling, psychotherapy, guidance, T-groups, church groups, and others is to assist individuals to function effectively in groups without loss of personal freedom. The primary concern of this chapter is an exploration of the development and processes of counseling groups; however, it will often be helpful to refer to other types of groups to elucidate further the dynamics investigated as well as the social significance of derived principles and theories. The counseling or therapy group, because of its exaggerated cohesiveness and intensity of emotional interaction, provides a kind of action laboratory for the study of the dynamics of other more specifically task-oriented cohesive groups. Similar dynamics occur in other groups but are more subtle and are less easily identifiable.

Counselors in schools and colleges work mostly with essentially normal people—adolescents and young adults. These individuals come to counselors, on a referral basis or self-referral basis in most cases, because of some sort of difficulty in interpersonal relations, often involving their membership, or lack of it, in groups. Some of these concerns would include (1) inability to make friends, (2) lack of popularity, (3) failure to find acceptance by the "right crowd," (4) a discomfort with the effect on individual development as a result of group identifications, (5) a rebellion against broader peer conformity pressures, (6) difficulty with older people, particularly in authority positions. One of the more frequently identified causes for early nonacademic dropouts in large universities is the sense of alienation felt by many of the residents of high-rise dormitories. These as well as other concerns seem most appropriate for a group counseling or group guidance approach.

The counselor who decided to use group processes in dealing with any of the above cited concerns would first need to decide upon an overall goal or direction. He *could* adopt the *adjustment* approach and, through group discussion, help the members realize that there really is not much one can do about the environment so the intelligent thing to do is accept and adjust to it. This approach usually involves the practicing of social skills and working through of interpersonal problems through roleplaying, sociodrama, lectures, and discussions of socially approved behaviors. The result, when successful, is a highly conforming social automaton. One would expect the recipient of this method to have considerable difficulty in maintaining his adjustment in a rapidly changing society.

The counselor *could* adopt the *openness* approach. Techniques are abandoned. The counselor stimulates the members to relate to each other at a deep emotional level with total openness and honesty of feeling and attitude. The situation is highly permissive, almost uncontrolled. The members are encouraged to express freely their innermost impulses and thoughts. Confrontation is common, presumably followed by acceptance. In some extreme examples, the situation takes on the appearance of an emotional orgy. One can scarcely argue the virtue of honesty and openness, but the generalizability of the behavior learned in such a group seems highly limited. Our social system is simply not geared to this type of behavior, and the individual who attempts it outside the counseling group may suffer severe rejection, and frequently does.

A third choice would obviously fall somewhere inbetween the two extremes just described, in terms of group structure and content of discussion. The point of compromise would depend on at least four important factors: the composition of group membership, the goal or intent of the counseling, the skill of the counselor, and the setting in which the counseling occurs. These factors will be referred to again at various points in this chapter.

THEORETICAL RATIONALE

The point of view toward group counseling presented in this chapter is better understood not as a compromise but rather a combination of the two extremes just described. A degree of management and control of the dynamics of the group is maintained towards social reality and at the same time individuality and creative (not simply explosive) expression is encouraged and rewarded. The management of the group's dynamic development is not held secret from the members. They understand the role of the counselor in this respect and it becomes an accepted part of the structure and norms of the group. *As the group progresses toward maturity, everyone accepts responsibility for group management.* This is not in itself an original conceptualization of group processes. *The uniqueness of this approach lies in the use of developmental stage model as a basic guideline of the progress of the group and the direction of its movement.* The level of functioning of the group during any given period should also help the counselor to determine his most appropriate modes of responses as well as provide him with clues as to the expected and/or desired succeeding developmental direction. The system may also be used as a means of identifying deviations from natural development and the reasons for these deviations.

Counselor's Role

As stated above, the counselor's major goal in the system described here is to assist the group toward a mature level of functioning. This experience is therapeutic in itself. Through the emotional support and courage derived from other group members and the counselor, plus direct meaningful interpersonal experiences, the individual member achieves the capacity to resolve much of his personal and relationship problems on his own. Deep insight may not be necessary.

This kind of group maturity cannot be achieved and maintained with stability except by progressing through certain growth sequences or developmental stages. Just as a child is not a "little adult," *neither can a group be considered mature at its inception regardless of the maturity level of its individual members.* Also, like a child, a group *may fixate at any level of maturity* short of creative interdependent functioning.

Although the primary function of the counselor is the management of the dynamics of the group, he must also respond to individual concerns and conflicts and neurotic entanglements between and among group members. At times an individual may express concerns or problems which are beyond the therapeutic maturity level of the group. At such times, the counselor may respond at length to the concerned individual or individuals almost as if the other members of the group were not present. *The group members soon learn to use these occasions as modeling-type learning experiences.* They perceive the importance of listening intently to all the client is expressing, and the significance of responding to his feelings with sufficient empathy to encourage further and deeper exploration. They also learn that content responses are intended to assist the client in clarifying the nature of his problem rather than attempting to solve it for him. These are obviously solid counseling principles. The importance in group counseling is that if the counselor even occasionally responds to individual group members in this manner, the other members soon perceive the impact it has and begin to react to each other in similar fashion. After the episode is completed or postponed, the material involved, the counselor's behavior, and the group's reaction to it can be brought back to group-centered discussion resulting in further maturational progress.

It seems evident, then, that the group counselor needs to be proficient in two major areas of knowledge and skill. He needs knowledge of the basic principles of counseling and the effective use of them, and he needs a thorough understanding of the dynamics of cohesive groups and the skillful management of them.

Developmental Stages

Before elaborating on the developmental stages of counseling groups and the dynamics one can expect to be associated with each, some brief definitions of central concepts will be given. The descriptions of the stages are based mostly on the writer's experiences with groups and supported by the experiences of his students. Other group counselors have found the system useful and not in violation of their own, often differing theoretical rationales.

There are three basic terms whose meanings need to be communicated clearly because they are so pervasive throughout the chapter and because their definitions and usage differ considerably when found in other contexts. These are creativity, cohesiveness, and group maturity.

Creativity. In this reference, the concept of creativity is a broad one and would involve divergent as well as convergent thinking, free and open expression of attitudes and feelings as well as ideas, the development and acceptance of novel approaches, and the willingness to alter the norms of the group when the needs of the task indicate it. This sort of group appears to develop, occasionally, rather accidently as a result of a fortuitous combination of personalities and events. Those interested in the dynamics of small groups have made considerable strides toward an understanding of these fortuitous combinations. Obviously, if we understand how this condition comes about accidentally, we can plan for its occurrence. (The need for this understanding has gone beyond the academic.) This use of the term creativity does not demand a resultant observable unique product, unless one wishes to conceive of a changed and more mature personality as a kind of production which may be emotionally felt and often behaviorally observed.

Cohesiveness. For cohesiveness to develop, meaningfulness and purpose and individual need gratification through the group's existence must be present. For the present discussion, cohesiveness may be defined as identification with the group by all members—a sense of unity, a feeling of "weness." Most of us have experienced membership in a cohesive group and know it to be a reality. We also know that nearly all people behave differently, as members of cohesive groups, from the way they perform when dependent solely on individual initiative or motive: frequently they behave more maturely but sometimes less so. People speak with pride about "my group." They often argue and fight over it, will even die for it, and show evidence of depression and confusion when removed from it. The composition and development of a cohesive group gives it an observable character which constitutes at least a phenomenal entity and a psychological reality. We perceive it and experience it as real; therefore it is.

Group maturity. We are all familiar with types of groups which represent differing levels on a group-maturity continuum. (The maturity of the group, however, is of greater significance than its cohesiveness, and it is also partially independent of cohesiveness.) A few examples of groups at differing maturity levels should make the further use of the term more explicit. The cohesiveness of a group may be based almost solely on interpersonal attraction or affection and sustained by a rather superficial common interest. Examples would be a housewives' neighborhood coffee klatch, a men's beer drinking group at the local tavern, and in most instances, college fraternities and sororities. Groups of this sort tend to disintegrate readily under duress or separation. The maturity level of such group identifications is almost infantile since it is so egocentric.

A second maturational level of group functioning might be best typified by a preadolescent boys gang or club. Rather severe initiations are characteristic, rituals soon develop, and a secret language or symbolism evolves. Loyalty to the group becomes the paramount virtue. The group exists almost purely for the sake of identification with a group and the motivational value is a sense of exclusiveness.

The similarities between preadolescent boys gangs and adult fraternal and civic organizations is surprisingly striking, particularly in terms of ritual, symbolism, initiation, and secrecy, all of which enhance a sense of exclusiveness and self-identity. The major difference is that, with the adult groups, a socially valued reason for existence, such as charitable or rehabilitative work, is usually considered necessary. Here, loyalty to the group and the importance of acceptance by the group will usually override purely self-centered motivations.

Athletic teams, particularly those which require a high degree of cooperation and mutual support such as basketball teams, move another step up the maturity continuum in terms of group functioning. Adolescent delinquent gangs possess nearly all the qualities of a maturely functional group except for the constrictions placed upon them by the nature of their anti-social goals. (The reader should keep clearly in mind that the emphasis here is on the maturity of group functioning not the maturity of the social value of the group's goals.) Planning committees, church groups, volunteer charity groups, local mental health societies, and many others of comparable intent may be functioning at any level on the group-maturity continuum regardless of their socially mature and noble goals.

The effective combat unit and the successful counseling or therapy group appear as the ultimate in functional, creative, mature groups. These groups must attain a high level of maturity or they cannot achieve their proposed or imposed goals. Other groups, such as committees or organizational units, can produce acceptably with something less than full cooperative effort. The counseling or therapy group and the combat unit may not even survive as groups unless they are able to achieve a full sense of interdependency.

As the reader may have derived from the preceding description of types of creative groups on a maturity continuum, cohesiveness may be attained on two major dimensions: interpersonal attraction and interpersonal respect. The balance between the two will determine the maturity of the group. Interpersonal respect would include respect for task-relevant skills, attention to expressions of individual ideas and feelings, and the right to individual and differing opinions.. If interpersonal respect is sufficiently well-developed, interpersonal attraction becomes relatively unimportant. However, some degree of original attraction is probably prerequisite for the development of respect. If cohesiveness is based almost solely on interpersonal attraction, it will inhibit task-relevant activities and thereby restrict the movement toward the preestablished goals of the group.

A Generalized Model of Small Group Development

A theoretical model is only an approximate representation of reality. In the behavioral sciences, the deviations from the model are usually more frequent than the replicas. A theoretical model of the sequential development of small groups can only be a very loose, generalized representation, for which there are many variations and exceptions. The variations and exceptions are themselves the most significant clues to the understanding of the dynamics of a particular group. The model proposed here should be regarded as a point of departure rather than a point to be proven.

Establishment Stage. When a group first forms, it has the same problem (multiplied by the complexity of the number of individuals involved) as a dyad in establishing a working relationship of whatever sort. The first stage—Establishment Stage—may be divided into two overlapping aspects: *exploratory and socialization.* During the exploratory or initial stage of the group, the members attempt to estimate each others' interpersonal impact and characteristic relationship modes. They further attempt to determine the kinds of roles they may play in this situation and still remain psychologically safe. Put another way, each individual estimates the emotional needs he may satisfy in interaction with the others without being rejected or overly exposed. The leader is often severely tested by the group in order to determine his orientation to the task and his leadership competencies. If the leader fails to meet this challenge, he may be rejected and psychologically isolated for the remainder of the group's existence or until such time as he proves his worth.

The chaotic nature of the initial phase of the group results in expressions of insecurity and leader dependency. Resistance and hostility toward the leader and conflict among group members are also expected outgrowths of the basic insecurity of procedural direction and uncertainty concerning the capacity of the group to achieve its proposed aims. The behavioral forms of these exploratory efforts are superficial social interchange (talk about the weather, current events, and job-related topics, intellectualizing the task, humor, apparently out-of-field behavior unrelated to the task, and general horseplay). All of this talk has a purpose and appears to be essential for group formation. If the group leader fails to recognize the significance and need for this kind of behavior, he may well lose the group before it starts.

Phasing into the second aspect of the Establishment Stage,

socialization, is characterized early by the distribution of "idiosyncratic credits" (Hollander, 1964), norm setting and consequent conformity pressures, and finally the first evidence of cohesiveness. The cohesiveness achieved at this point appears as a warm, congenial, social atmosphere which may be, to some extent, camouflaged by superficial task efforts. Interpersonal attraction is often at its height at this stage, but somewhat falsely so. The cohesiveness represents the warm glow of achievement at having successfully managed the first hurdle in the formation of a psychological group. The members know now that they can cope with each other and function at some level of significance. Some groups never move beyond this point and accomplish little that is meaningful as a group or for individual members.

Hollander's concept of "idiosyncratic credits" is the process by which the group, consciously and unconsciously, assigns power and influence, in varying degrees, to each member of the group. It represents the extent to which each member will be allowed to deviate from the group norms. Some group members may be granted extensive idiosyncratic credits while others receive little or none.

Closely associated with the distribution of credits is the concept of "norm setting." Norm setting may be defined as the group consensus of the limits of allowable behaviors, which includes the variable reward values for behaviors within the limits and the punishments extended for behaviors which exceed the limits. As the group norms are formed, pressures are exerted for each member to give evidence of his conformity to them. In this manner, each member may develop some broad definition of what he may and may not expect of the other members.

The leader's behavior during the Establishment Stage is in some ways similar to the behavior of the members of the group. He, too, attempts to estimate the developing roles and positions of the members of the group, and what he can expect of them in relation to himself. At the same time, the group is working very hard both subtly and directly to anticipate and formulate the role of the leader. The leader must be very alert to his role assignments by the group. He needs to accept the right and need of the group to express their concerns and demands, and should respond to them with reflections and limited or relatively superficial interpretations. This will naturally lead to some loose definition as to his perception of his role in the group. At this point, he may very likely be asked about his qualifications for the task. His answers should be direct and honest but very brief and concise. Through these kinds of interchanges, he will have fulfilled the group's need to test his competency.

The leader should assume an active though not highly directive part in the formation of the group's norms. Ideally, the setting of norms should emanate from the group itself; however, if certain issues considered vital by the leader, such as confidentiality, are not broached, the leader should suggest to the group that these issues be given some serious consideration. The eventual acceptance of a group norm should still be left to the consensus of the group and not forced by the leader, particularly in the early stages of the group's development. If a group determined norm is unworkable, it will soon become evident to them and subsequently altered. The leader may influence openly or subtly, to a limited extent, the types of norms developed. The extent will depend upon his acceptance as a leader.

The following protocol of an audio-taped group session is presented as an example of the dynamics of the Establishment Stage. The group is composed of young adults. Norm-setting, with particular reference to confidentiality, is the focus of the group's attention. The protocol is an excerpt from the third session.

    Establishment Stage Protocol—Norm-setting, Confidentiality
    D.—Last Monday, when I went home, I went home and I said to my wife, "Well, we had our group tonight." And she said, "Oh, you had your group." (*Laughter.*) Anyway, I decided I couldn't tell her a thing about it; I couldn't tell her a darn thing, even things I wouldn't consider breaking confidence—like mentioning names—not even incidences. It might be the beginning of starting to tell about somebody. Yet, there is the need to want to share things. You know, with my wife. Who else can you talk to? I didn't tell her anything. I'm wondering how the rest of the group felt about this. What can we say and what can we not say? What are our rules for not breaking confidentiality?
    Th.—Well, uh, well first have any of the rest of you had a similar reaction?

E.—I did. I think maybe because we had a good group session. By the time I drove an hour I had overcome some of this. (*Group laughter.*) I had the same feeling of wanting to share it with someone else.

J.—I didn't want to share it with my husband; I wanted to share it with someone in the group.

D.—I could risk this in individual therapy because I'm just talking about myself then; but when I tell about a group, it's not my province to tell. But yet there's a need to want to talk about it to somebody.

Th.—Would you like more clarification about how we ought to deal with this—where the limits are?

R.—I think it becomes a question of who. I've come to the conclusion it's better not to say anything, except with other members of this group. I feel when the session is over, everybody just kinda stands around, like they want to continue. Anybody else feel this way?

G. & J.—Yeah. Yeah.

R.—Is this wrong to discuss with someone else within the group?

Th.—This is encouraged by some group therapists, but this could be difficult for some of you to do, like if you have a husband or a wife, you may be expected to come home—could lead to difficulty.

P.—As far as D.'s concerned, this might have particular significance for you if you want to have a closer communication with your wife—talking about these things might give you a chance to air some of your own feelings.

D.—Yeah, yeah, that's right. I usually tell her just about everything, but I came up to this point where. . . . Gee, this is nothing spectacular; you're not going to tell on all these people. But I thought, "Why should this be different?"

Th.—I don't suppose anybody in this group would object to your telling your wife. I doubt if anyone here would object to your telling her anything that happened here—in last week's meeting, but there may come a time when things would occur here that they would not want you to tell even to your wife.

D.—Sure, they don't know her or who she is!

Th.—Or who she might blab to.

D.—Right!

Th.—Well, I think you will do some of it; people usually do tell some things. I think within a few weeks you will have developed a sensitivity to what's all right to talk about and what isn't. But to expect you to be absolutely closed-mouthed about this and never mention it to a soul is kind of silly because you probably will. One thing that might help you, D., particularly if this is something that has relevance to your marriage—I know people have done this and

I have done this—to say to your wife or someone pretty close to you, "Something came up in our group discussion tonight that I think might be of interest to you and me." And then not repeat what was in the group discussion, but take off on the topic, "We had a good discussion of marital relations between two people who are both professionals and some of the problems that might arise from this. Let's continue it; I'd like to talk with you about it." And then you're not repeating anything; you're just bringing up the topic which is the point you are trying to make anyway.

D.—Right!

Th.—Not that you want to repeat what's been said.

D.—Right!

Th.—Or if you say, "I had an insight in the group tonight. I found a new way of looking at some things and I would like to talk to you about it." Then you are talking about your insight, not anything the group said. That's all right; that's good, if it stimulates you to do things like that. That's one of the things we would hope to get out of this.

Th.—Does that seem acceptable to everyone—as a way to deal with it?

Group—(*nodding of heads—seemed unanimous*).

B.—I agree. It's a very difficult thing to build up this emotion in the group and then suddenly drop it.

Th.—I think you're right, and you probably shouldn't. But you can, I think, develop ways to release it without feeling you have broken confidence.

Transition Stage. With a group of mature individuals or a group of individuals in serious need of problem resolution, the social stage of cohesiveness soon wears thin. The realization comes through the instigation of one or more group members or from pressure from the leader that the group is not seriously pursuing the goals for which it was originally formed. If the group as a totality accepts this recognition, it enters into what has been termed the Transition Stage. If the majority of the group members are not ready for this recognizance, the group will likely revert to its original chaotic state and soon disintegrate, if circumstances allow it to do so.

Transition has its usual implication here of a critical period of movement from one developmental stage to another. The group feels a sense of embarrassment at having pretended task-relevant behaviors for which they had little commitment coupled with a sudden lack of confidence that they can actually accomplish the original group aims. If the group has maturity potential, it will reevaluate its purpose, re-form its norms, and determine to try again at a deeper and more intentional level.

The counselor's behavior during the Transition Stage is of vital importance to the continuation of the group. The nature of this stage has been described as a state of incongruity (Bonney and Foley, 1963). The members of the group (especially adults) have learned that it is socially unacceptable, if not dangerous, to discuss deeply personal problems in a group, particularly a group of strangers or mere acquaintances; yet this is the reason for the formation of the counseling group and the presumed intention of every member in it. The reluctance to discuss personal concerns is referred to, by some writers, as a "basic social fear" of group rejection (Bach, 1954). The counselor can relieve the conflict and the anxiety associated with it by accepting and agreeing that withholding personal concerns in normal social groups is not only understandable but probably wise. He then redefines the counseling group as normatively different and therefore appropriate for the discussion of personal concerns. The very nature of the norms they have established and are still in process of establishing protect them from the dangers inherent in the normative structure of more usual social and work groups. The counselor's acceptance of the conflict and his clarification of the purpose of the counseling group stimulates the group members to more serious norm development and group commitment.

The following protocol, taken from the sixth session of an all-female group, is included here to illustrate the Transition Stage. The problem discussed is typical of the concerns of the Transition Stage. The group seriously questions its capacity or willingness to be truly helpful and resolves to accept the challenge.

Transition Stage Protocol

E.—I think we just felt concern talking about your problems when you weren't here. I didn't feel that we talked of anything much—mainly because two of us were missing.

D.—My main concern was that we hadn't *helped* P. when she had asked us for help.

G.—That's what we discussed, why we hadn't helped and just how we could go about it.

P.—I guess that's how I felt afterward. What is that old Indian saying? "Don't judge me until you have walked a mile in my moccasins!"

E.—I've had problems similar to yours, but I still didn't feel I could tell you what you should do. As far as the group is concerned, I don't feel we have come along far enough to tell each other what they should do.

D.—I think the thing that surprises me the most was E. thinking that I was mature. I thought I was falling down on my part and E. saw it altogether differently.

P.—This is the one thing that concerns me, too. I get the impressions from Mrs. C. [therapist] that we should just let go! And I think that E.'s holding back looks like a sign of maturity. (*Directed to therapist.*) Well, I think that you feel that we hold back too much!

Th.—I think the point I would like to make is that this is different from any other kind of group. We can only understand each other and therefore help each other by talking openly.

D.—I feel that we turn away from each other's problems, because we are embarrassed or we don't really feel that it's real or whatever. What we need to realize is that whatever we do say is significant in some way.

Th.—P. wasn't particularly asking you for advice; she was asking you for understanding. Just by the mere fact that you stay with a person and listen indicates that you are concerned. And this is the way that you are going to be able to work with each other.

E.—Oh good! I'm glad you said that. Now, I don't have to solve her problem. (*Laughter.*)

D.—Just listen carefully and try to understand.

E.—It also makes a difference how we state our problems. If I say it as a joke, the group will laugh at it.

Experimentation Stage.   Having successfully passed the Transition Stage, the group enters the Experimentation Stage in which the first serious attempt as a group is made at goal-related work. These first attempts are often highly tentative, sometimes blundering, and fraught with interpersonal conflict and frustration. The difficulties encountered at this stage of development are mostly due to one or more members who were not quite ready for the transition or who did not completely understand the new norms of the group. If the conflicts or the frustrations become severe enough, the group will have to engage itself in a second transition or *Retransition Stage.*

Many groups fail to mature beyond the Experimentation Stage and never become creative groups. Some individuals lag behind or actually impede progress while a few do most of the group work. The typical committee tends to function in this manner. If the goal is sufficiently well-defined and specific, the group product can still be quite acceptable. However, if the goals are not easily specified, such as in a counseling group, or are extremely threatening and difficult for some members, such as in a combat unit, a sense of frustration will continue and satisfaction with the group will be minimal.

Early efforts by an individual member at serious self-exploration are often hesitant and confused and he may need considerable assistance from the counselor in organizing his thoughts and expressing his feelings more clearly. These early efforts should be strongly reinforced by the counselor but he should also be very cautious that he does not push the client too fast. The client may reveal more than he intended or can later tolerate, and the other group members may be threatened by it and withdraw from further participation. The interpersonal conflicts and frustrations should be allowed to work themselves through. If this working through is not at least partially accomplished within a reasonable length of time, then the Retransition Stage becomes necessary. The counselor responses to these conflicts and frustrations should be simple reflection and clarification, and possibly some interpretation.

The following protocols are taken from two different adolescent groups and present two of the more common developmental difficulties during the Experimental Stage. Both examples represent the tentative, approach-avoidance nature of this stage.

The first excerpt is an example of a group ready to accept and, in fact, pressing the client for depth exploration; the client is unwilling to pursue it. The second excerpt is an example of a client willing to explore himself in depth but the group is unwilling to permit it.

Experimental Stage Protocol—First Group (College Freshmen), Eighth Session

(At the end of the previous session, R. had stated he thought he should talk about his father. The counselor has invited him to do so.)

R.—Well, I can't really see how my dad could have influenced me. I wasn't brought up by him. I didn't get any of my ideas from him. The only thing I've learned from him is the type person I don't want to be. Really, no reason to talk about him.

Co.—You really feel you have no feelings about your father now.

R.—Except I wish he were different.

E.—You feel cheated?

R.—No, I'm glad he left.

Co.—But, every time you mention your father, you have always appeared upset. It seems like it might be important.

R.—O. K., I'm ashamed of him.

Co.—You haven't been able quite to bring up anything really personal.

R.—I think I could if I really wanted to. (*The counselor withdrew and turned to another client.*)

It is not uncommon, in this stage, for a client to announce his intentions to explore a personal concern, then become quite inhibited and withdrawing once he has started. In this instance, the client may also have been resisting the efforts of the counselor to draw him out.

Second Group—High School Seniors, Sixth Session

Co.—Does anyone feel like starting today?

B.—Yes, I want to talk about my fear of trying new things. I make myself try things and I usually do all right, but I'm so afraid beforehand. Like last summer, I was a camp counselor and I did O. K., but I was miserable for weeks before it started.

Co.—What's so different about that? Doesn't everybody feel that way?

F.—Sure, I've felt that way lots of times.

B.—I know other people feel that way, but I feel like I'm more so.

Co.—Seems like what you're saying is that this fear is controlling your life.

B.—Yeah! It prevents me from looking into things or being openminded.

Co.—Prevents you from knowing what you *can* be.

P.—Uh, Huh!

B.—Yeah!

F.—But, after you've shown some ability in something, it doesn't bother you anymore. I would feel that way too, and you can do things I can't do.

B.—Yeah, but there are some things I really get so afraid of I just don't try.

P.—But still you do a lot of things even though you are nervous about it.

B.—Well, yeah!

The client, B, was attempting to explore his feelings of anxiety and timidity at a greater depth than the other group members were willing to accept. They tried to reassure him that he didn't really have a problem. During the session, the group finally understood what he was trying to do and supported him..

Retransition Stage.   During the Retransition, the group members reexamine their position and attempt to identify the sources of their difficulty in achieving their assumed potential. Emotional commitment and genuine concern of all members is soon identified as the missing and necessary condition. Direct individual confrontation is a typical means of attempting resolution. Interactions are highly charged emotionally and often accusatory and defensive. Regression to former stages of resistive behaviors is typical. The group members seriously face the possibility that they may not be capable of achieving the task of full cooperative, creative functioning. If the interpersonal conflicts are resolved and full commitment obtained, the group moves into the Operational Stage of development.

Operational Stage.   In the Operational Stage, all group members function at a task level and evince respect and support for the efforts of all other members to behave similarly. Each member's contributions are given full attention and are considered seriously in respect to the overall aims or goals of the group. If a group member's contribution falls short of expectation, the others confront him with this and attempt to help him achieve a higher level of functioning. From here, the group phases into the final or Creative Stage of *full interdependency.* Even here, interpersonal conflict is not uncommon, and occasional regressions to earlier developmental stages are to be expected. However, resolution of difficulties is almost assured, even though the process may be traumatic and stormy.

The following brief excerpt from the eighteenth session of an adult group represents the kind of serious, searching efforts of the Operational Stage.

Operational Stage Protocol—Self-exploratory

M.—Then this caused me to begin to think, "How did I look at myself?" I look at myself, first of all, as mother, second of all as . . . um . . . I guess as good old M., but never as a woman.

Th.—And felt you had to deny that in order to function in these other ways?

M.—No, I don't think I denied it. I just didn't believe it.

J.—Kinda afraid to, too. . . .

M.—Might be, but I don't think I really believed it. I'm not sure I believe it yet. (*Several somewhat irrelevant interchanges among the group members followed this comment.*)

M.—I don't have a feeling of hopelessness now as I had before. I feel I can be a valuable person, I guess, without having to be valuable in things I do—be valuable for what I am. I'm still trying to talk myself into it, but I'm intent on it. I'm working at it. (*At this point the group members understood and became quite accepting and supportive of M's efforts to reach out for something more in life.*)

Creative Stage. During the Creative Stage, the counselor responds almost solely to group centered dynamics. The group members have learned to deal with each other in a therapeutic, open manner with little or no reservation or unnecessary protectiveness. Because of lack of experience and their own highly emotional involvement in the process, they are usually unable to resolve and sometimes even recognize a total group dynamic which pervades everything they attempt to do and inhibits efforts to deal with each other as individuals. The counselor must now identify the nature of the dynamic for the group, trace its origin, and help them resolve it. An example of a total group dynamic might be an unrecognized or unconscious reaction to the previous group meeting. The group just cannot seem to *get going,* but they do not know why.

In this ultimate or creative, self-actualizing stage of the group's development, dependency upon the leader is negligible.

He is used now primarily as a resource person or for emergencies of gross confusion or very severe interpersonal conflict. A full sense of interpersonal responsibility and group commitment has developed which allows for and rewards idiosyncratic behavior. To break the norm constructively has become the norm. In this atmosphere, one can learn to become a responsible individualist while functioning fully as a member of a cohesive, task-oriented group.

FACTORS AFFECTING DEVIATIONS FROM THE DEVELOPMENTAL MODEL

The major factors which are likely to affect deviations from the model are the combination of personalities within the group, the goals of the group (guidance-discussion, focused counseling, open counseling, depth therapy), conditions and events outside the group, and unexpected and unpredictable events within the group. These factors are stated in terms of counseling groups, but a very similar list worded differently would apply to other small cohesive groups as well.

A student counselor, under supervision with the threat of a grade, would probably try to accomplish too much and too fast to the detriment of the group's progress. One would expect he would have his greatest difficulty at the first Transition Stage. The total possible time that a group can spend together most probably influences how long the group will remain at one stage of functioning. The end of a semester or school year or the deadline for a committee report are examples of this type of influence. The physical setting and the meeting time can have some influence. A meeting time just prior to some very different kind of demanding situation, such as an academic class, will limit the returns from both experiences. Highly unique factors could arise which might exert some minor deviating influence. Occasionally an unusual occurrence can have a major impact, such as the death or psychotic breakdown of a group member.

The major forces toward progression or regression arise from the interpersonal dynamics within the group and the individual motivation of each member for group-centered goal achievement. This latter concept has been referred to, in reference to the training of rifle squads, as Team Task Motivation (TTM) (George, 1962). TTM is, to some extent, developed according to the summation of task-relevant or goal-relevant skills of the group members, but more basically, it appears to be dependent on the attitude toward group participation which each individual brought with him from his early past experiences, most likely rooted in the nature of the family relationships during his early childhood and his position in the family constellation. Group-centered motivation could probably be fairly well estimated through a carefully structured interview prior to the formation of the group.

The interpersonal dynamics of the group refers to the mutual pairings, the cliques, and the personality clashes that inevitably develop in any cohesive group. The extent to which these interpersonal encounters can be managed for the enhancement of group effort rather than its delimitation will determine the success of the group experience and the course of its movement from one developmental stage to another. The successful management of these interpersonal dynamics is related to the extent to which they are neurotically based and to the skill of the group leader. These two major aspects of the group's development, individual attitude toward group participation and interpersonal dynamics within the group, are closely interactive. It is often difficult, and sometimes impossible, to separate them observably.

Earlier in this chapter, the suggestion was made that deviations from the model presented here could provide interesting clues to understanding the nature of a particular group and the prediction of the group's future progress. One can also often use the deviations of the group from the expected pattern as leads for developing more effective managing techniques. For instance, if the group progresses too rapidly, skipping certain developmental experiences, the leader might anticipate severe transition problems later. Goal preparation and anticipatory experiences prior to the formation of a group appear to alter the expected pattern and produce some unique management problems (Foley and Bonney, 1966). An example familiar to all group counselors is the psychologically sophisticated, therapy-wise group member who starts too fast and at a depth which threatens the other group members and impedes progress. In a similar manner, an "Old Army Pro" assigned to a squad of relatively inexperienced men can wreak havoc with the leader's control and the general morale, or he may, under favorable conditions, prove to be an invaluable asset to the development of the group. He may play the role of a secondary resource person. The same could be true of the sophisticated member of the counseling group.

There are other factors which may alter the developmental pattern. Familiarity of all group members with one another prior to the group formation will usually facilitate movement up to and through the Transition Stage. Familiarity among some members but not all will often make progress difficult and sometimes impossible. The relationship of group members to the leader outside the group is usually a hindrance rather than a help. The intent and skill of the leader is of vital importance. It is certainly not unheard of for leaders of many types of groups to seek a leadership role in order to satisfy their own neurotic needs for dominance and control rather than goal achievement or individual development. The inept leader, no matter how appropriately motivated, may also impede group progress. The highly skilled and goal-oriented leader can often overcome or resolve relationships with individuals which would tend to mitigate against progress of the group.

Many individual gains are possible through participation in an evolving, creative group experience. The usual lists of personal improvements as a consequence of involvement in cohesive groups seem valid and evident. Some of these benefits would include the use of the group as a source of consensual validation of social and emotional reality, an increase in the skills of interpersonal techniques, an extension of one's role behavior repertoire, a greater tolerance for differing opinions, and more appreciation for the value of cooperative effort. Beyond these usual claims, the mature group may also provide the participant with an increased sensitivity to individual, interpersonal, and group dynamics, and a new perception of the meaning and necessity for human interdependence. One might expect that he would develop a deeper appreciation of the horizons of human potential and the significance of interpersonal encounter as a means of realizing individual potential. Most important, one might hope that the participant would achieve a more profound understanding of the meaning of maturity through the development of a deeper sense of interpersonal responsibility.

SUMMARY

This chapter attempts to promote a conception of the significance of group counseling within the social structure of modern American society. The counseling group, as well as some other small group endeavors, may be approached as a kind of training experience for individual and creative expression within a cooperative group effort. We need very much to learn to work cooperatively in groups without loss of individualism. Group counseling may well be the type of laboratory setting in which we can learn most about how these complimentary goals may be best accomplished.

The chapter proceeds with a consideration of two extreme types of group approaches which were termed *openness* and *adjustment*. This was followed by a suggested combination of the two extremes as the encouragement of individual expression within the confines of reality based group management.

The meanings of group maturity, cohesiveness, and creativity were discussed and illustrated. The stages of the development of a counseling group were identified, discussed, and represented by illustrative protocols. The developmental stages were identified as *Establishment, Transition, Experimental, Operational* and *Creative*. Finally, a discussion was presented of the meaning of deviations from the developmental model.

REFERENCES

Bach, G.: *Intensive Group Psychotherapy*. New York: Ronald Press, 1954.

Bonney, W. C., and Foley, W. J.: The transition stage in group counseling in terms of congruity theory. *Journal of Counseling Psychology*, 1963, *10*, 136-138.

Foley, W. J., and Bonney, W. C.: A developmental model for counseling groups. *Personnel and Guidance Journal*, 1966, *44*, 576-580.

George, C. E.: *Some Determinants of Small Group Effectiveness.* Research Memorandum, Human Resources Research Organization, Fort Benning, Georgia, 1962.

Hollander, E. P.: *Leaders, Groups and Influence.* New York: Oxford University Press, 1964.

SUGGESTED READING

Bion, W. R.: *Experiences in Groups.* New York: Basic Books, 1961.

Schutz, W. C.: *FIRO: A Three Dimensional Theory of Interpersonal Behavior.* New York: Rinehart, 1958.

Stock, D., and Thelen, H. A.: *Emotional Dynamics and Group Culture.* Washington, D. C.: National Training Laboratories and New York University Press, 1958.

Tuckman, B. W.: Developmental sequence in small groups. *Psychological Bulletin,* 1965, *63,* 384-399.

VII

FAMILY GROUP CONSULTATION

DANIEL W. FULLMER

T HE FAMILY REPRESENTS the cultural social system. Congruence between family and culture is one measure of emotional health. The Family Group Consultation method of group counseling uses cultural discrepancy within a family to measure (estimate) adequacy. Whether a family is healthy or unhealthy may remain ambiguous because it is difficult to make qualitative evaluations of the discrepancy between the two systems; there is more potential, however, in delineating the similarities and differences between the family social system and the cultural social system. The typical counselor's day includes working with children who are products of inadequate family social systems, i.e., from families that fail to represent the cultural social systems.

More than eight years have been committed to the development of Family Group Consultation as a method of group counseling, and in this method, a number of assumptions are made about behavior, how it develops, and what it means.[1] This chapter represents an attempt to share with the reader the essentials of Family Group Consultation.

OVERVIEW: DEVELOPMENT OF, AND CONDITIONS FOR FAMILY GROUP CONSULTATION

Family Group Consultation is a method for learning, teaching, and treatment. It is a method of group counseling; a treatment for those families in need of help. It is also a method for family education and even counselor education. Any one of the several

---

[1] The author has a film and a file of cases which illustrate the degree of success achieved through the method. Additional testing and experimentation in a cross-cultural setting also has been initiated.

purposes may be the reason for using some form of family involvement in the treatment process in school counseling and guidance.

Even though there are numerous methods for family counseling (MacGregor, Ritchie, Serrano, and Schudter, 1964) employed by several professional persons on the national scene, still Family Group Consultation is new to the 1960's. The initial effort began as an attempt to find a productive model for working with school referrals of the University of Oregon's Medical School. Patients were referred for child guidance from the schools through the standard types of community and social agencies. These patients ranged in age from fifteen years to adult. However, when the families were seen, younger children also came to the sessions. Following one year of development, the program was moved to the Counseling Center for Adults at the Portland Extension Center, Oregon System of Higher Education. The method began as an effort to find a more productive model to use in schools with children identified as having learning and/or behavior problems, and it has continued to be developed as a method for use in the school setting involving all ages or any array of ages.

Family Group Consultation is a way of working with all of the significant persons concerned with a given child. There are many appropriate ways of working in the elementary and secondary schools, but the Family Group Consultation method unifies the efforts of all the persons concerned with a particular child. This method accommodates a wide range of possible groups where much latitude for working is provided. The children, parents, teachers, administrators, and specialized personnel may constitute the group. The number of sessions should be adapted to the demands placed upon the situation. Some families are helped from a single session, while some families require help for a year or more. As a rule, six to twelve sessions are required to produce good results.

The key personnel in all family consultation is the "convening authority" group. The school people themselves are the prime movers. The school counselor creates an arena in which all persons concerned with teaching and learning have access to each other. Because the classroom is a convenient model for teaching, it provides an acceptable arena for most families. Learning results from repeated and continuing dialogue among the significant professionals, parents, and children.

Irish (1966), in reporting a study of Family Group Consultation, pointed out that the arrangements are as follows: from one family up to four families (up to eighteen persons, the ideal is ten to twelve) meet together in the same room with two or more counselors. All family members and/or significant other persons are encouraged to be present. A table and chairs are preferred in order to approximate a family at dinner. The group runs for one and one-half to two hours. The experience *together,* over a period of time, forms the basis for subsequent sharing among the counselors and the family members. All data are gathered on the scene in the all-at-once, here-and-now milieu. Structure is imposed upon the ambiguous mass of the data as it is collected. This keeps the projections and interpretations of meaning open to challenge, expansion, clarification, and validation by everyone.

ASSUMPTIONS IN FAMILY GROUP CONSULTATION

Family Group Consultation makes a number of basic assumptions. These assumptions are outlined below.

Assumption One

Learning is more important than is teaching. Most of what a person must know to understand the meaning of his existence is not taught by anyone. It is learned from being with other persons (Hall, 1959). Human behavior is learned only in groups. Only in groups is there reason to share our learning (humanity). The group, therefore, is *both* a learning and teaching model. The family—a living group—is the most pervasive model for learning and teaching provided by the culture (Mead and Heyman, 1965).

Bernstein (1964) speaks of restricted codes in the form of communication learned within a family and within a specific social class. The code sensitizes its users to specific forms of social relationships in family and community experiences. These were not taught, but caught. Bernstein's purposes in psycho-

therapy are somewhat similar to Family Group Consultation—
that of learning *new* behavior. The "teaching" is done through
social relationship instead of by teacher-classroom methods.
The teaching function becomes a communications function.
The learning function includes more than what is purposefully
taught (Fullmer and Bernard, 1968).

Assumption Two

The family is the model for learning used by the culture.
The culture is represented by the family and is perpetuated
through the learning occurring in the family. The mentally
healthy family is an example of the cultural model at its best.
The less healthy family is less able to achieve the goal of producing healthy, fully functioning children and adults.

Learning within a family goes on in the absence of direct
teaching. The learning of significant behavior and the rules
regulating the expression of behavior are a part of what Hall
(1959) has called the Informal Culture. The Informal Culture
is not verbalized nor made explicit except as the person learns
the rules and behaves in the real-life arena. Loukes (1964) says
we "catch" our skills and knowledge in the community of other
persons. Thus, it becomes a truism that we should be as concerned with the process of how a person comes into his knowledge as we are with the content of what he learns.

The family medium lends support to the idea that informal
culture has to be learned but is not usually directly and systematically taught. If it is caught in the community with others,
there is a significance to the idea that a person's most important
learning is not taught (Culkin, 1967). As an individual, one
learns the culture from being in it. Culture and community
merge at the point of a family—a living group.

In American culture, almost all rules governing human behavior are found in the informal culture (Hall, 1959). Formal
culture is taught by admonishment and precept. The technical
culture is explicit and easily verbalized, therefore teachable.
Not so with the informal culture—therein, we have the focus
for family counseling as conducted by the method of Family
Group Consultation.

Assumption Three

One is unable to understand someone else until he can comprehend the other person's meaning. Meaning must be understood in terms of the "other" person's social system or personality. Errors will result from any attempt to extract meaning from someone's life experience if one uses his own social system to interpret *for* another (Kemp, 1967).

On a person-to-person basis, the counselor searches for the source of meaning in the life of a family because it leads inevitably to the meaning for an individual family member. The person seeks to behave in response to the system of valuing he uses. The system or process of valuing leads to a system of beliefs. The meanings, beliefs, values, valuing, and culture are each related to one's comprehending the other person's interests and concerns. With insights derived from understanding the family, the counselor can start the process of influencing another's behavior. To change behavior, however, the counselor must begin with his own understandings.

Assumption Four

The personality pattern of an individual is shaped within the social system of his family. Handel (1965) supports this basic idea with the results of his studies of families. The child becomes what the parents are. The most widely practiced behaviors in a family's social system (society) provide a key to the character of that family.

Behind the behavior of every person is a hidden agenda of meanings. The meanings and their system of beliefs comprise the warp and the woof of the fabric of human personality and character.

The person *is* the way he behaves. Each person creates his uniqueness and finds expression of his meanings through his behavior. Uniqueness requires variations of specific behaviors and beliefs (values).

Assumption Five

Knowledge gaps within a family's social system are perpetuated on a generation-to-generation basis. Likewise, knowledge and skills in managing behavior and social issues, newly acquired by a family, will be perpetuated on a generation-to-generation basis. The educational function of Family Group Consultation is maintained by this foundation principle.

A family is defined by the system of moral obligations which commits the members to each other and to society. When responsibilities and expectations consistent with the culture are instituted within the family, the moral obligations are learned by the child. Within the highly organized, healthy family, tight interpersonal loyalty exists. Therefore, there are few knowledge gaps, and what is learned in the organized social systems of the family transfers to the organized social system of the culture.

Disorganized families are sick families. Children in disorganized families do not learn to function in ways that transfer to the larger community. Conflicts are not resolved and the build-up overburdens the family members, whereas the conflicts in the organized families are resolved without disorganizing the members. Interpersonal conflicts within a family are similar to the conflicts encountered in the community and social system outside the family. Adequate and adaptive social behavior can best be learned in a healthy family.

Assumption Six

The family pattern of management for the forces that shape behavior becomes more a fact of the family social system than of individual choice. In order to change the social control over individual behavior, the child must separate himself from the family's control. If he attempts this, he may establish *another* family. However, a cycle of patterns emerges: the *new* family is much like the older one with the major exceptions being in the role assignments. The former son becomes the husband; the former daughter becomes the wife. Again, the system is shaped. The pattern of forces in the *new* configuration or family social system repeats the basic assumption for generation after generation. Once a family social system has been shaped, the system shapes the personality of each individual in the family. The limits and possibilities for behavior become set by each family system. The pattern of forces available to the individual includes those forces that release or nullify his potential and enhance or hinder expression of his behavior (Bronfenbrenner, 1967).

The foundations for this assumption come from several disciplines. Psychology helps to explain the impact of reinforcement schedules contained in the family pattern of behavior, circumscribed by the social system outside and within the family. Anthropology offers the explanation of culture in terms of formal learning—the learning without teaching of significant rules in the informal culture, and the systematic teaching and learning of the technical culture. Education gives us a methodology for developing strategies to share knowledge and skills of the formal culture and the technical culture.

Family Group Consultation is an attempt to describe, define, and teach the informal culture rules of behavior by the process of learning-how-to-learn. Learning-how-to-learn is the process used in acquiring a system of beliefs and a method of thinking. Behavior is the expressions of the meanings one person has or a group of persons share. The system of beliefs and the method of thinking used by a person is a partial description of his personality. To make the individual conscious of these meanings is the process of learning-how-to-learn. The purpose is to help the person know what he knows in any given here-and-now life arena.

Assumption Seven

Human behavior is equivalent to a communication system. Symbolic representation is clearly coded if one can learn the isolates and sets that comprise the pattern of behavior for a person. Language is used to communicate about behavior, and thus to clarify the meaning of the silent signals. In order to learn the meanings for an individual, we need to distinguish between the explicit verbal communication about behavior and the behavior messages themselves (Watzlawick, Beavin, and Jackson, 1967).

Each family can be viewed as culturally different from all other families. Such a statement is more a measure of the problem present in family work than it is a measure of the solution. The statement, "I cannot understand," may mean, "You speak to me from an alien culture"; or "Your words don't fit your behavior patterns." The ramifications of this idea are the subject of concern with disadvantaged persons when referred to as culturally different.

The culturally different person cannot learn until the medium is culturally similar. As a teacher, one can teach only culturally similar persons, because what has been learned *before* is not relevant to the *now* of culturally different persons. The system of beliefs for the teacher and students must be alike. Actually, their "culture" is learned on the spot. The teacher teaches by learning. However, the knowledge that the teacher *shares* was not previously known. One may not teach as much as he learns, but as he learns a new system of beliefs, he shares through his behavior. The wisdom to share is probably the oldest known to mankind—learn together.

Assumption Eight

A child learns character from being a member of *his* family over a long period of time. The other reinforcing behaviors repeated by each parent and other children create a schedule for shaping habits of response, attitudes or values (morality), and system of beliefs such that they last a lifetime. Each child learns to anticipate his own impact in interaction with other family members. Later, he learns about his impact in peer groups, play groups, and still later, in work groups. Thus, the person learns about his behavior and how to adapt to each new situation.

The child becomes in character what the parents really are in character. It is not what I say to my son, nor what I do; it is what I *am* that he will use to guide his becoming a man.

The child is *indeed* father of the man. If we look closely at the model the child is using, we can see the process happening. It is not unusual to witness the formation of behavior in a family member in Family Group Consultation. The newly formed behavior is the communication.

The family is the place where the child learns who he is, what he is, what he may become, and how valuable he is to self and society (Irish, 1966). A family may need help in fulfilling this function. The school is one institution among many formal social organizations concerned and involved with creating fully socialized persons. Family Group Consultation was developed to provide a method for preparing school counselors who could become significant helpers of children, youth, teachers, and parents. Because the family forces are so pervasive an influence upon the child, the assumption is made that only through direct intervention with the family, and significant other persons in the life-span of a child, can school counselors interrupt self-defeating behavior patterns in school youngsters and institute a pattern of systematic influence on behavior modification through new learning of more productive coping behavior (Fullmer and Bernard, 1964).

The task is difficult unless a counselor can achieve a significant relationship with the person to be influenced. The family provides the counselor with one means of achieving this relationship. It is with people significant to him that the child learns what it is to be a person. Phrased more directly, to modify my behavior, you *must* influence changes in persons significant to me. I am influenced by "others" through their regard for me. Their behavior, over time, tells me how I am regarded, what I am worth, and what is expected from me. Then I learn what I should expect from myself. I *always* try to meet expectations from myself and others. Expectation is the primary source of standards for one's behavior in our complex culture.

The condition essential to create a situation that permits my behavior to change is insufficient in and of itself, because I must learn, under systematic teaching conditions, some new behavior. It is necessary for me to practice the new behavior under special and safe conditions in order to incorporate the modifications into my repertory. Feedback from significant other persons will help me adjust and adapt refinements in understanding and skilled functioning. The programs of reinforcement are resident with the behavior of others with me. Behavior rewarded under such schedules will be self-perpetuating (Chein, 1962).

The reader should note that what is being described is a self-conscious process of learning in an experiential (emotional and cognitive) real-life arena. The real-life events created by counselor intervention in family functions provides situations in which significant learning occurs. Staying in the situation over substantial periods of time supplies the life-forces that influence behavior modification. Thus, there is no tool or technique except the counselors themselves as the "models-of-the-possible." The principle is stated as follows: Give me time with you and I will influence your behavior, and you will influence mine. So, we learn together, over time, to practice, to experiment, to evaluate, to interact, and to incorporate new behavior into my repertory, and you incorporate new behavior into your repertory.

Assumption Nine

Symbolic representation of meaning is a purely human characteristic. Because of this, we send many messages simultaneously with the possibilities of many meanings; therefore the possibilities for confusion are present.

Human culture arises out of that condition in man which allows him to symbolize his meanings. Therefore, an infinite leeway has developed to permit allowances for the other person's being. An "Informal Culture" emerged to accommodate this condition in man. The hope is to make explicit the unverbalized messages and meanings each individual lives with in his life-space (Mahl, Danet, and Norton, 1959). The nonverbal and noncontextual behavior constitutes a message system that constantly qualifies the meanings being communicated verbally. One example is that the words of a taped speech are no substitute for a face-to-face encounter.

PROCEDURES IN FAMILY GROUP COUNSELING

The procedures used in family group counseling, according to the consultation method, are described below.

Initial Session

The initial session consists of supplying information and helping the family get acquainted with the physical arrangements and the psychological procedures of Family Group Consultation. Factual information such as ages, interests, occupations, concerns, and other identifying items and criteria can be collected. Second, information based on an interpretation of behavior is obtained. Interpretation consists of descriptions of events concerning the interpersonal life of members within a family and the occurrence of interaction between family members and external agents—persons from other families, or persons in work groups or play groups.

Although the initial session is used primarily to gather information, information gathering continues in all subsequent sessions. The family members observe that the counselors make use of the information on the spot. They also learn more about themselves and about the learning process. The incidental nature of information gathering following the first session emphasizes the importance of the initial session since the emphasis or concern with the nature of the information gathered in subsequent sessions shifts from factual (identifying information) to the interpretative-descriptive type.

Each family member is asked to respond to a question, "What issues are before this family?" In turn, each person reports how he sees himself in the family and explains the role that he plays in each significant family situation. Closure is achieved in this line of questioning when each member of the family has responded to the qualitative question: "In what way are you important to your family?"

All family members need to attend the consultation sessions if the family is to be unified. However, it is not uncommon for only a few members to be present in the initial session. In addition to family members, all other persons significant to individual members of the family are urged to attend the Family Group Consultation sessions. But we take the attitude that we will work for a brief period of time with whatever part of the family is available to us.

There are limits to how much can be accomplished with only part of a family, but each counselor needs to discern for himself the benefits of working with a part of a family as compared with the entire family. Counselors may consult each other as team members during each session as well as following each session.

The counselors keep a careful record of the members present

from the nuclear family. They also are careful to delineate the relationships that appear between the mother and father, between mother, father, and the individual child, between and/or among siblings, and all of the possible combinations of the above. These data supply the basis for the counselors in helping them determine who controls the family. The decision is based tentatively upon the apparent kinds of involvement each individual family member demonstrates, e.g., who talks for himself, and who talks for the family. The interaction sequence of who talks for the individual and who talks for the family is also observed. Who talks for whom becomes a criterion for making the assessment concerning the controlling member of a family. The absent member may also control by withholding his participation.

In addition to the verbal exchange in Family Group Consultation, other cues such as facial expression, physical activity, autistic activity, body posture, and intonation of voice are interpreted by the counselors in conjunction with the verbal exchanges. This is the reason for maintaining that each counselor must be aware of his own bias in relation to the interpretations he makes of other people's behavior. Another way of stating this is that one must learn to read behavior as a language of messages and meanings.

In summary, from the initial session, the counselors achieve an estimate of the involvement of each individual in a family group. The estimate is based upon assessment of loyalty, alliances, and interpersonal contracts maintained within the family. It is necessary to form some hypotheses concerning the kind, amount, and influence of the involvement of each individual in relation to each of the other individuals in the family group. This is a considerable task but must be performed in the initial session.

The initial session and all subsequent sessions are divided into two separate forty-five- to sixty-minute meetings. During the first meeting, all parents and youngsters meet together in the same room with the counselors. It is recommended that, for the second meeting, the group be divided into two parts. This division is for the purpose of separating the children from the parents thus enabling them to feel freer to discuss their concerns. The parents also experience less difficulty discussing some topics when their children are not present. The counselors note the change in behavior and in relationships among the children in the absence of parents and vice versa. Some items as physical freedom, the ability to verbalize, and the inclination to discuss topics not discussed in the presence of parents (or children) are all examples of items to be noted by the counselors. A goal of Family Group Consultation is to get parents and children to learn to discuss together any and all concerns—without a mediator.

Session Two

In the second session, the systematic process of discussing the basic issues and concerns of family members is begun. Counselors become mediators who listen as family members interact. This is a complete change of behavior on the counselors' part when contrasted with the initial session.

The second session should occur no more than one week following the first session. The counselor may open the session after initial greetings with, "How has it been going?" A brief lead and a general question allows family members to determine the topic for discussion. The initial response will be closely related to social protocol and may go something like this, "Well, we went over to see Aunt Mary last night." The counselors then lead into more productive material including interpretation of behavior which occurred while the family was visiting Aunt Mary. What sorts of things transpired between them and among family members, and how each felt about the experience, constitute a major focus of the second session.

The special significance of a life event on the part of each individual member of a family can be determined if the counselors will carefully check the following events including the pre- and post-elements: What happened just before the event occurred? What was your contribution? What was the contribution made by each person in the event? Next, the counselors investigate what happened while the event was taking place. They ask each person, beginning with the one relating the story, the following questions: What happened? What did you do? What did each person do during the event? Finally, the counselors gather information on behavior following the event. They ask: What happened? How did it go? Who did what? What did you do? What did each person do? What happened as a consequence of the event?

Out of this material, the counselors begin to get a pattern of loyalties, alliances, and contracts existing within the family and with members significant to the family. The counselors continue to check out with each member of the family what the relationship patterns really are on the dimensions of loyalties, alliances, and personal contracts. The dialogue in the second session is such that counselors participate only in terms of checking out what is being said to be sure to sift out the relevant meaning concerning certain patterns of behavior. These behavioral patterns are determined from material put together in answering the following questions: What goes on in this family? What is it like to be a member of this family? How would one feel if he were a member of this family? What would life be like? What meanings would one have in this relationship setting?

A further example of the kind of relationships counselors study is exemplified in the mother-son relationship. A mother may be observed as trying to meet her son on his terms and asking the son for his loyalty in the form of a symbiotic alliance. To further check this hunch, the counselors listen closely for any evidence that would indicate the mother had disqualified herself as his mother in the eyes of this son when she attempted such a bargain.

The counselors also carefully explore the possibility that the mother knows the nature of her relationship with her son. In one such case, in response to a counselor's query "What would you do?" the mother pleaded "Please, tell me what I should do." (*The counselor should always avoid a direct response to such questions for information and description.*) The real purpose of the query has been served if the mother does not countermand the counselor's estimate of the nature of the relationship.

Validation of the suspected mother-son relationship can be established based on information obtained in answer to the following queries: Does the son actually defer to this relationship? How does the son utilize the power he has over his mother? Does the mother receive a payoff from the relationship that she is reluctant to exchange or give up in response to some alternative plan that might be evolved in the counseling relationship?

A basic principle that is adhered to in all family counseling is as follows: First, and foremost in all behavior, and therefore in all counseling, counselors must be supersensitive to the need for allowing each person the privilege as well as the responsibility for owning (taking title) his own behavior. To have answered the mother's question would be tantamount to sharing ownership of her behavior. To respond to her behavior with the questions, Who holds the title to your behavior? and, Whose behavior do you hold title to? could focus attention upon the basic criterion, Who owns the behavior? *Responsibility must be left with the owner of the behavior.* Accountability must be left with the significant group—the family.

Rather than answering her question, the counselors might proceed by asking her to talk about the alternatives available to her. They might ask her, What other possible ways of behaving have you thought about?; or How do you think a mother *should* act? If the mother were unable to respond to the counselors' queries, the group is then utilized and questions are directed to them for discussion. In this way, the mother listens to other persons making statements about what they think is possible, and thus they share with the mother ideas from other points of view which otherwise might be unavailable to her. This is the process of consultation. A person has established access to others. The person is able to select and use what he wishes.

The second session, as are subsequent sessions, is used to give the members of a family extensive practice in reporting the behavior of themselves and others in the life events of the family. (We have found the learning to tell one's story to be a significant skill.)

Session Three

During the first two sessions, the counselors have accepted

secondhand reporting of events in the lives of the members of the family. At the beginning of the third session, it is essential that each individual utilize the pronoun "I," rather than he, she, or they, as an event is related or as the story is told. This effort allows for the principle: "Each person must become owner of his own behavior." His own behavior is the only behavior over which he has any *direct* control. Each one must be permitted to speak for himself.

By using the pronoun "I," the focus of the report is kept upon the individual recounting the event. The counselors must be alert to discourage parents or siblings from correcting one another and adjusting the story that an individual wants to tell. "This is your idea, now we want to hear Johnny's," is one way to discourage such attempts. With the focus on the person who is recounting the life event, the person is encouraged to assume title to his perceptions of events; the use of the first person singular is a constant here-and-now reminder. Descriptions of the identical life events by each member of the family permit the counselors to formulate hypotheses concerning the patterns of behavior within a given family.

As one family relates its story, other families listen. Each individual is given a way of validating his perception of a life event by listening to the varying reports from other persons concerning a similar event. Through a series of meetings, individuals within the different families acquire experience together. The experiences that they have together become another source of confirmation in the continuing trek toward a mutual concept of behavior validation. The perceptual content of the reports and the individual's verbal exposé of his experience allows for this kind of multiple level dialogue within Family Group Consultation. It is one of the unique methods of modifying behavior. (The process of behavior validation is the method used to teach persons how to *use* help. How to *get* help from other persons is the second phase of treatment.)

During the third session, each individual within each family should begin a kind of evaluation of his own behavior. By the third session, there are multiple opportunities for an individual to express an awareness that other families also experience difficulties and problems and that the kind of problem he experiences is not necessarily unique to him. By the end of the third session, families are expected to have established a firm commitment to the idea of consultation as a method of learning and one which holds possibilities for the family as a group as well as for the individual members. They become aware that more work in Family Group Consultation will need to be done in learning and perfecting the methods of feedback and perceptual modification as well as learning to tell the story of the family. Learning to tell the story becomes a central issue by the beginning of the fourth session.

Session Four

The most obvious item of behavior demonstrating commitment to Family Group Consultation is regular attendance. Due consideration must be given to absent members for legitimate reasons; however, it is generally understood that the persistently absent member of a family is usually closely connected to the basic problem under discussion. The counselors must assume the responsibility for exposing covert concerns, and this includes confronting directly any member of any family with his poor attendance record. The following types of questions may be put directly to him: Why do you come here? What is the purpose in your coming? What purposes are served by your coming? For whom do you come? The answers to any one of these questions may provide some clarification of each family member's status of attendance.

Further evidence of commitment can be gained from the extent of active participation in the process of family consultation. If someone has maintained a position of listener without any apparent pathology or any apparent resistance, the counselors should reevaluate the nature of the member's condition for participation. They can do this by checking the adequacy of descriptions offered by individual family members and the estimates obtained from counselors' observations over the first three sessions.

The counselors then reflect to the family members any consistency or discrepancy they pick up so that it may be clarified by some kind of rebuttal from the member in question. This is handled by simply making the query, "I see you behaving this way; I wonder if that is the way anyone else sees you?" Also, "How do you see it?" The feedback that the counselors give to the participant forms the basis for another kind of dialogue that goes on in family consultation. The member of a family is free to agree, disagree, or clarify the perceptions of the counselors. At times when the counselor(s) "owns his statement," the member of a family is helped to "assume title to his statement."

During the fourth session, individual members also are encouraged to focus upon themselves in relation to other members. This activity is the most complex expected in family consultation. The individual must state his concept, clarify the relationship between his input and the other person's input, and assess the output on the basis of a set of values and a way of valuing (a way of thinking). This complex kind of interaction is particularly difficult when the other persons concerned are present and are able to check the validity of the story. The highest level achieved in family consultation on this dimension is that point in time when the individual can accurately assess his input, the input of others, analyze the relative meaning for each person involved, and confront himself with discrepancies in his own behavior. The person who achieves this level is considered able to learn by his own efforts. He has a basis for knowing what it is he knows. The confirmation and validation, as always, must come from others.

The lack of commitment to the Family Group Consultation process may be characterized by individual members who tend to wander from one topic to another without focusing for any extended period of time or any depth on a given issue. The wandering should become the issue so far as counselors are concerned, and the member should be confronted with the question focusing upon this observation. The nature of the question might be in the form of a statement of the observations, such as: We don't seem to be able to focus on any one subject today; I wonder what is happening. The counselor's interjection of this observation allows for some further assessment of the commitment from individual members within the families. By the end of session four, each person should have the process of consultation learned and operating—namely, an internal reference to self in relations with others, rather than external problems about self and others.

Session Five

By the time the fifth session is underway, the members of the family groups will be able to use some of the counseling skills they have learned in Family Group Consultation. The idea of owning the perceptions of behavior through the use of first person singular, "I," helps to establish the possibility that an individual will have learned to focus upon the outcomes resulting from his relationships with other people. Focusing upon these consequences with due regard for the feedback from other persons constitutes the significant force operating in a learning-how-to-learn situation. Making self-conscious the process of learning concerning the informal culture, as described by Hall (1959), constitutes a major step in the direction of establishing successful conditions in family consultation.

A principle, which sometimes begins operating as early as session four, is concerned with meaningful communication. It is exemplified by the stated principle "I cannot understand the communications of another person until I understand his meanings." The essential aspect of this concept relates to what happens without it. If the counselors interpret the meaning of a life event of another person in the terms of the counselors' own perceptions, values, and meanings, it will be at variance with the meanings experienced by the other person.

The concept of communication between the sender and the receiver of messages constitutes the major emphasis in the evaluation and feedback system utilized in family consultation. The attempts at clarification of meaning between the signal sender and his receiver continue as a check and balance system throughout all sessions of family consultation. Some attempts to clarify are as follows: What did you say? What did it mean to you? What did it mean to the other person? How does the other person respond to these meanings? Does he 'consense' or does he contest the interpretation given by the other person?

Specific life events, such as incidents happening within the group of families during consultation, serve as the proving ground for the validation of accurate communication. Because counselors and family members experience the incidents together, their consensual validation provides the beginning for an accurate assessment of perception and meaning. The process of clarification of this meaning is basic to the communication system in Family Group Consultation. Family members learn how to do this without the mediation of the counselors. The behavior transfer of this kind of interaction becomes paramount to the success of family consultation.

Family Group Consultation is not complete until the family members can actually interact with one another apart from the counselors. This means that an individual within a family has learned to give feedback to each person in the family setting and also to evaluate and validate behavior and meaning of each person in the family setting. Once this has happened to the satisfaction of the significant other persons in the family, it is a signal to terminate family consultation.

Each individual will have been asked to look at his own behavior and then to look at behavior of others in the situation in response to his signals—his output. Sessions should continue for six to twelve meetings following the procedure outlined above. If, after twelve meetings, people are not ready to terminate, they should be encouraged to take a furlough from family consultation. In the school setting, it is not desirable to extend sessions indefinitely. Because of limited time and the press of other business, it is essential to utilize the concept of a terminal group; six weeks or eight weeks is enough to commit to one group of families. In order to hold to this formula, the counselors should contract with the parent groups to meet with them regularly for five, six, seven, or even eight sessions, after which there will be a termination of the group. Contracting also is suggested as an antecedent condition to consultation in order to avoid the open ended continuing of a desirable relationship.

Further Sessions

The sessions from the fifth to the terminal session constitute essentially the same procedure. In these sessions, the identification, description, and clarification of problems confronting the individual families continues as a central theme. The principle that all families encounter problems at all times is assumed in Family Group Consultation. The concern is whether the problem confronted by the family actually handicaps the family in its operation in other areas. The healthy family has been described as one which can function in all other areas even though the members have a drastic conflict occurring in a specific area. By contrast, the unhealthy family or sick family is incapacitated in all areas until the conflict in a single area has been removed.

In terms of a dynamic society, such as our American western culture with its urban industrial complex, the possibilities for producing persons who are capable of productive behavior are enhanced by the healthy family. This is an assumption with some merit in terms of our educational system. Productivity is a goal. Productivity is defined as any and all behavior enhancing to self and/or others. Idea production is closely associated with the goals of education. The healthy individual can *think* and *act*.

A focus upon possible alternative ways of behaving is central in the procedures and the processes of family consultation. The sources of these alternatives range from individual member to members of other families and counselors. Individuals and families are encouraged to practice, on a try-out or experimental basis, new alternatives, i.e., new to their milieu. They are then asked to report back to the group what happened. Again, the "event analysis" procedure—what happened before, during, and following, and who did what, when, and to whom—is used. The final evaluation questions are always, How did it turn out? What will you modify next time?

The group is helped to learn how to summarize what has been going on, how it has been proceeding. The family in this way learns to use the summary as a way of evaluating progress and a way of establishing the criteria for planning the next steps in their procedures to learn more.

The final session is concluded with the recommendation that

the family seek further discussion either by phone or in person
if they see the situation as requiring it. Certain key questions
are included as a method of helping to keep a communication
process open and operating in the family. Before termination,
it is established whether or not the family is practicing talking
things over at home within the family in ways similar to those
used in family consultation. They are asked whether they can
use similar tactics outside their family in resolving conflicts and
differences and gaining information and validation for their behavior in other groups. Each family is in consultation with every
other family. As a result of this, each family is asked to suggest
things to other families in circumstances similar to their own.
The counselors are always concerned with the strategies that
each family has learned to employ in order to maintain its more
healthy functioning relationships (Watzlawick, *et al.*, 1967).

GOALS OF FAMILY GROUP CONSULTATION

The linguist says that any conscious thought can be put into
words. The anthropologist says that the rewarding discovery
of a pattern of behavior from a culture is a matter of having
"put it in words."

Informal culture, as described by Hall (1959), is not verbalized and it lies beyond the conscious awareness of persons
brought-up in the culture. However, those same persons are
most aware of informal culture violation. It is outside of their
verbal awareness. The rules governing informal culture are not
explicit. To make explicit (verbalize) such rules, is to initiate
"instant learning" in a group of persons "native" to the culture.
The reason is simply the fact that natives know it already
because they learned it while growing into adulthood—even
though they were not "taught" the informal culture.

The informal culture is "caught" by each of us as we live
together with persons significant to us. This explains at once
why we are so concerned about the company we keep and the
companions our children have. It is a tragedy for a person
who has no one who "cares" for him. He cannot "catch" the
informal culture—the pattern of behavior essential to learn

integrated behavior within the society. Such a person is in conflict with society. He is then ostracized and permanently denied access to models and events from which he *could* learn. The conventional wisdom of "He has lost out" has much factual material in it. The opposite of this occurs when an informal pattern is adequately described all-at-once in the here-and-now of behavior. Other persons from the same culture understand immediately because they have learned it previously (Hall, 1959). A goal of counseling is to make the informal culture of rules to live by explicit by putting it into words and, therefore, easily learned even by those who were denied a healthy home. This is the first task or goal of Family Group Consultation, and the first task in person-to-person relationships.

Another goal of family consultation is to make explicit in expression through the informal culture the patterns of family and individual behavior. Partial or incorrectly analyzed patterns of behavior will result in confusion for all concerned. One must teach only when the technical descriptions fit the facts in real life situations.

The power of Family Group Consultation as a training model lies in the revealing of the rules and codes the counselors use in living through informal patterns of behavior. A counselor needs to learn to read his *own* behavior before he can learn to read the behavior of someone else. Counselors question whether we should work with families. They are questioning whether the violation of informal cultural taboos, assumed to be in existence, should be sanctioned by the school. Of course the question is always legitimate, but I ask you to look at what it means. What follows from the various assumptions made in the answer *no* and in the answer *yes* applied to the above question?

COUNSELOR'S ROLE IN FAMILY GROUP CONSULTATION AND SOCIAL CONTROL

The counselor's role in Family Group Consultation can perhaps best be described by means of the analogy of a teacher-student conflict situation. I am a teacher of seventh-grade social studies. A boy acts out in violation of the culture (you pick the event); what is my response? Is my biology comfortable or distorted and physiologically painful? *My behavior will follow my feelings!* If I can keep the facts straight—namely, that my response (to be determined) *is my* behavior—I have a choice. The boy's behavior belongs to him. I am then less vulnerable to my *own* biology. This will give me time to *think* and feel. What is happening? What is my input, here and now? What is the boy's input? Later, I can worry about the rest of the class. Now, eternally now, I am concerned with keeping straight the ownership of behavior.

If I communicate clear title to all behavior, what will happen? First and foremost, I will be under my *own* control, not under the control of the boy's behavior. This is a *significant difference.* The power to act stays with me instead of being dependent upon the boy's next act. I am *not* asking him, "Please, behave in a way I can accept." Such an act would give my power to the boy.

Social control is always central in school discipline (La-Mancusa, 1966). Any youngster wanting to express something may obtain an audience (not just get attention) by violating the school culture in a small way. For example, the boy or girl may omit the Mr. or Mrs. or Miss before the teacher's name. "Hey Jones" or "Sally old girl" are examples. Maybe "Hey stupid" will disarm the teacher. To call for a redress of the grievance against *respect* is to pass my power to the youngster. Control of *my* behavior response *must* stay with me. If my biology gets upset I will be very uncomfortable. If I become uncomfortable, I will demand a change of behavior from the youngster. I am now trapped by a demand: Change your behavior to something I can accept. All a youngster has to do is refuse, and I am faced with a need to act-out. If I act-out, my behavior becomes similar to that of the boy.

It can be seen from the above analogy that the counselor has the responsibility of being in control of his behavior and assisting his counselees to assume titles to their behavior.

In summary, the counselors' (always a team of two or more) roles in Family Group Consultation are similar to mediators or referees. The formula for reporting a life event is an example.

The clients, in turn, are asked to express their internal or personal story about their participation in an event. Their perception of what happened is carefully revealed in the presence of each of the other participants and the counselors. The round robin reporting results in a unique configuration to reveal the patterns of behaving so essential to the counselors' understanding of the meanings being communicated within the family. Confirmation, accuracy, discrepancy, and congruence emerge in bold relief. The counselors must insist that each family member be given the mandate to "speak for himself." Like the recurrent themes and styles used to identify the works of creative artists, the recurrent phrases in family consultation reveal the neurotic distortions, redundancies, paradoxes, and conflicting emotions. From such revelations as these, the counselors may discover the meanings used within a family.

COUNSELOR QUALIFICATIONS FOR FAMILY GROUP CONSULTATION

The sheer power of natural groups like a family, even disorganized families, makes Family Group Consultation a group procedure with many pit falls for the neophyte counselor. It is not a diagnostic and clinical method for school counselors but it is a treatment-learning method. Clinical skills are useful in Family Group Consultation, but it requires approximately two years for otherwise fully qualified school counselors to learn these skills from an expert under usual Family Group Consultation conditions. The chief limitation, then, of this treatment-learning method, is reflected in the counselors' lack of clinical expertise in working with small groups and the length of time through "tutorial" methods that it takes counselors to become educated in the method.

SUMMARY

The family is a complex group. A group may evolve as a social system. If it does not, the group may disorganize. We all assume that we know a great deal about the family as a group. Yet, do we know enough?

1. The family is the one group where our behavior supports the idea that learning is more important than teaching.
2. All children learn in all families. What is learned by the child is a consequence of the family social organization, manipulation of forces, and the unique reactions of the child.
3. Healthy families produce healthy adults.
4. Sick families cause children to be handicapped in many ways.
5. Family living is the controlled exposure of a child to life experiences and, consequently, to learning. Controlled development follows as a second concern in the process of growth toward adulthood.
6. Learning is a process; behavior is the content and the consequence of what has been learned. In order to learn, what conditions must prevail? In order to change behavior, what conditions must exist?
7. Behavior is a display of what has been learned. The system of beliefs will qualify the behavior acted-out in the here-and-now.

Learning-how-to-learn is the key to the culture. Knowing-how-to-know is the key to behavior validation. Knowledge of this will help to answer the following crucial questions in Family Group Consultation:

1. In order to learn, what must happen?
2. In order to change behavior, what life conditions are necessary?
3. In order to pursue Family Group Consultation,
   a. what conditions must prevail?
   b. what behavior changes must take place?
   c. what learning is necessary?
4. In order to generate new behavior, the person must generate new action and communication—how is the family uniquely equipped to create?

REFERENCES

Bernstein, B.: Social class, speech systems and psychotherapy. *British Journal of Sociology*, 1964, *15*, 54-64.

Bronfenbrenner, U.: In A. S. Makarenko: *The Collective Family: A Handbook for Russian Parents*. New York: Doubleday, 1967. (Translated by Robert Daglish.)

Chein, I.: The image of man. *Journal of Social Issues*, 1962, *18*, 1-35.

Culkin, J. M.: A schoolman's guide to Marshall McLuhan. *Saturday Review*, March 18, 1967, *11*, 51-ff.

Fullmer, D. W., and Bernard, H. W.: *Counseling: Content and Process*. Chicago: Science Research Associates, 1964.

Fullmer, D. W., and Bernard, H. W.: Family consultation. *Guidance Monograph Series*. B. Shertzer and S. Stone (Eds.), Boston: Houghton Mifflin, 1968, No. 9-78820.

Hall, E. T.: *The Silent Language*. New York: Premier Books, 1959.

Handel, G.: Psychological study of whole families. *Psychological Bulletin*, 1965, *63*, 19-41.

Irish, G.: Behavioral changes of participants in family group consultation. Unpublished doctoral dissertation. Oregon State University, 1966.

Kemp, C. G.: *Intangibles in Counseling*. New York: Houghton Mifflin, 1967.

LaMancusa, K. C.: *We Do Not Throw Rocks at the Teacher!* Scranton, Pa.: International Textbook Company, 1966.

Loukes, H.: Passport to maturity. *Phi Delta Kappan*, 1964, *46*, 54-57.

MacGregor, R.; Ritchie, A. M.; Serrano, A. C., and Schudter, F. P.: *Multiple Impact Therapy with Families*. New York: McGraw-Hill, 1964.

Mahl, G. F.; Danet, B., and Norton, N.: Reflection of major personality characteristics in gestures and body movements, 1959, Yale University Research, United States Public Health Service Grant M-1052.

Mead, M., and Heyman, K.: Family. New York: Macmillan, 1965.

Watzlawick, P., Beavin, J. H., and Jackson, D.: *Pragmatics of Human Communication*. New York: W. W. Norton, 1967.

NAME INDEX

209

SUBJECT INDEX

A

Activity group counseling
activities used in, 61, 63, 66, 67, 70
and counselee behavior, 75
and play techniques, 61
and research of, 66-70
and the school environment, 70
counselor's role in, 74, 75
definition of, 61
effects of with disadvantaged Negro
    boys, 68, 69
effects of with junior high school
    problem boys, 69
ground rules in, 73, 74
new application of, 62
peer reactions in, 62
pioneers in, 62
rationale for behavioral change
    through, 70-73
selection of group members for, 76,
    77
size of groups in, 77
suggested readings in, 85
with disadvantaged Negro boys, 67
see also Activity group therapy
Activity group therapy
a type of group therapy, 30
pioneer of (Slavson), 63
research of, 63-66
with adolescents, 66
with adult mental patients, 65
with delinquent boys, 64
with delinquent girls, 63-65
with hospitalized youths, 65
see also Activity group counseling
Adlerian group counseling, 12, 13, 17,
    29
Alienation (sense of), 158, 159
American Journal of Orthopsychiatry,
    32
American Personnel and Guidance
    Association, group procedures

interest group of, 8, 18
Assertive training, 43
*A Teaching Program in Human
    Relations and Mental Health,* 27

B

*Basic Approaches to Group Psycho-
    therapy and Group Counseling,*
    xi, 31, 45
Behavioral counseling
focus of, 120
related research of, 131, 132
theoretical principles of, 120, 121
see also Behavior modification,
    Behavioral therapy, Social
    learning, Reinforcement
    learning
*Behavioral Counseling: Cases and
    Techniques,* 137
Behavioral group counseling
behavior dealt with in single units,
    140, 141
counselor's role in, 142-145
different from other theories, 152
goals of, 137-140, 145
group composition in, 146-149
limitations of, 149
rationale, 129, 130
related research of, 131-133, 148
relationship in (value of), 144, 145
selection of counselees for, 138, 139,
    146-149
sex factors in, 148
student's (counselee) role in, 145,
    146
techniques of, 141
termination of, 142
uniqueness of, 137-143
See also Reinforcement counseling
    and Group counseling

213